21
DAYS TO
Jump-Start
Your
Intuition

Also in the 21 Days series

21 Days to Awaken the Writer Within
by Lisa Fugard

21 Days to Become a Money Magnet
by Marie-Claire Carlyle

21 Days to Decode Your Dreams
by Leon Nacson

21 Days to Explore Your Past Lives
by Denise Linn

21 Days to Find Success and Inner Peace
by Dr. Wayne W. Dyer

21 Days to Master Numerology
by David A. Phillips

21 Days to Understand Qabalah
by David Wells

21 Days to Unlock the Power of Affirmations
by Louise Hay

21 Days to Work with Crystals
by Judy Hall

21 DAYS TO

Jump-Start
Your
Intuition

Awaken Your Most
Empowering Super Sense

SONIA CHOQUETTE

HAY HOUSE

Carlsbad, California • New York City
London • Sydney • New Delhi

Published in the United Kingdom by:
Hay House UK Ltd, The Sixth Floor, Watson House,
54 Baker Street, London W1U 7BU
Tel: +44 (0)20 3927 7290; www.hayhouse.co.uk

Published in the United States of America by:
Hay House Inc., PO Box 5100, Carlsbad, CA 92018-5100
Tel: (1) 760 431 7695 or (800) 654 5126; www.hayhouse.com

Published in Australia by:
Hay House Australia Pty Ltd, 18/36 Ralph St, Alexandria NSW 2015
Tel: (61) 2 9669 4299; www.hayhouse.com.au

Published in India by:
Hay House Publishers India, Muskaan Complex,
Plot No.3, B-2, Vasant Kunj, New Delhi 110 070
Tel: (91) 11 4176 1620; www.hayhouse.co.in

The information given in this book should not be treated as a substitute
for professional medical advice; always consult a medical practitioner.
Any use of information in this book is at the reader's discretion and
risk. Neither the author nor the publisher can be held responsible
for any loss, claim or damage arising out of the use, or misuse, of the
suggestions made, the failure to take medical advice or for any material
on third-party websites.

A catalogue record for this book is available from the British Library.

Tradepaper ISBN: 978-1-4019-7609-5
E-book ISBN: 978-1-83782-115-0
Audiobook ISBN: 978-1-83782-114-3

10 9 8 7 6 5 4 3 2 1

Printed in the United States of America

This product uses papers sourced from responsibly managed forests. For
more information, see www.hayhouse.com.

*This book is dedicated to my beautiful
granddaughter Sufiya Rose, whose Spirit
jump-starts my joy every single day.*

Contents

Publisher's Note

Research has shown that establishing a habit requires 21 days of practice. That's why Hay House has decided to work with prestigious authors to create the *21 Days* series, designed specifically to develop new mastery of subjects such as jump-starting your intuition.

Other titles that will help you to explore further the concepts featured in the 21-day program are listed at the beginning of this book.

Introduction:
An Exciting Awakening

Intuition is our natural sixth sense, and moreover, it is a super sense. It's our internal guide, radar, protection, truth serum, connector, inner light, and the voice of our Higher Self. It is our inner hotline to our angels and Spirit guides and the Divine Mother-Father God who loves us unconditionally and forever. Intuition is the Divine intelligence we all possess that helps us find our place and fulfill our purpose in this magnificent and holy Universe that we live in. Intuition shows us how to make everything we imagine and yearn to create possible. It leads us away from situations, things, and people that do not serve our highest good and toward those that do.

We are all naturally endowed with this super sense; centered in our heart, it radiates out through every cell in our body, communicating the wisdom of our Spirit through vibration. As spiritual beings, we are designed to follow this guiding inner light to live up to our full potential and fulfill our purpose. It is a natural and essential part of our basic human operating system. It is not an optional sense or a gift bestowed upon some and not others. We all possess an intuitive super sixth sense and need it to succeed. Experiencing a profoundly satisfying, purposeful life becomes nearly impossible without our intuition guiding us. Like any elegant system, our lives cannot work well with essential pieces missing.

Being disconnected from our intuition is like trying to find our way through a dense, fierce jungle at night without a flashlight and with no protection. It leaves us in the dark and at the mercy of our limited, frightened, overreactive, and misinformed egos. We become stressed and suspicious of everything and everyone around us. Without our inner guiding light to reveal the world's true nature, we often become defensive, drained, and depleted. We lose our way and futilely struggle to find our security and sense of worth in the approval of others. We distrust and abandon ourselves, feeling we can only find safety by pleasing those we perceive to have power over us, leaving us feeling disingenuous, exploited, betrayed, wounded, and angry.

Our intuition frees us from this free-floating anxiety and uncertainty and connects us to our authentic natures. It keeps us safe and protected. Without this super sense at the helm of our lives, guiding us as it is designed to do, we end up living far beneath our fullest potential, often missing open doors of opportunity, ignoring our true callings, and focusing only on surviving as opposed to thriving as empowered, creative, and joyful Divine beings.

Fortunately, unlike the other five senses, we cannot lose this super sense. It exists as the Divine life force beating in our hearts. We must simply jump-start it back into action so it can work its magic. Fortunately, this is easier than you might think, especially if you take it a day at a time. By introducing a gentle prompt to awaken your dormant intuition each day, after only 21 days, your super sixth sense will spring back into full force within your heart and cells, guaranteed. When this occurs, the joy and magic of life return. That is precisely what this guide will help you do. So, without further delay, let this exciting adventure begin.

Week 1
TUNE IT

This week we will jump-start your intuition by first recognizing what it is, noticing what it feels like in your body, understanding where it originates, and creating the ideal conditions for your intuition to wake up and leap into action as it is designed to do. You will discover and activate an exciting superpower you didn't know you had and start to put into practice what will quickly become your greatest asset and support forever.

DAY 1

Reclaim Your Missing Piece: Intuition

The first step in awakening your intuition is recognizing that you are a spiritual being naturally designed with six, not five, senses. The sixth, your intuition and super sense, is essential to your spiritual anatomy. It is hardwired into your cells and connects you to your authentic Self and Divine support system. It is not an optional sense. It is essential to success in every area of your life, and without it, you are more likely to lose your way, be controlled by fear, and fail to achieve your highest potential or experience deep personal peace.

All human beings experience intuition through various subtle vibrations, but it is not "one size fits all." Some people sense their intuition with a quiet rumble in the gut or a buzz up the back of the neck. Others may feel intuition as a deep inner knowing in their heart or a chill up the arms. Others receive intuitive messages in their dreams or experience sudden "downloads" while doing the dishes or washing the car. Intuitive sensations are familiar to nearly everyone because they are hardwired into our nature, just as birds have migration intuition, bats have echolocation, and whales have sonar to navigate. We have our inner guidance system too. But while most people may ignore these valuable signals, the intuitively awakened person pays attention. Still, noticing intuitive feelings is not enough. Countless people notice their intuition yet still dismiss it, shooing it away as if it were something wrong, calling it "weird" and "woo-woo" and shutting it down. This is like closing your eyes in traffic or ignoring the smell of fire in a building. In other words, missing this powerful inner protective sense is self-destructive.

Your intuition keeps you safe and guides you toward what is good for you and away from what isn't. This is because intuition makes you aware of what the five physical senses cannot register. Intuitively awakened people not only sense their subtle intuition but listen to it. They look for intuitive signs and signals, and follow their guidance. They check in with their subtle inner compass and trust what they feel, even if it cannot be immediately logically explained. They know in time it will be.

People everywhere spontaneously tune in to their intuition because it is necessary for survival. The world is evolving so quickly, the old systems collapsing so fast and new ones popping up at dizzying rates, that to navigate all these wild changes, we need all our natural senses to be on board and engaged, and especially our sixth super sense.

Even scientists are beginning to recognize that we have more than five senses because we are more than just physical beings. The field that studies this phenomenon is called quantum physics. Simply put, everything vibrates as energy, even us. Our five physical senses recognize what is vibrating in the outer, slower, dense physical plane, while our sixth sense tunes in to what vibrates faster on the energetic quantum plane. Just as it is vital to follow the feedback of our five physical senses to avoid walking into traffic or escape a burning building, so, too, is it essential to follow our subtle sixth inner super sense, our intuition, to stay safe, connected to our authentic Self, and moving in the direction of our highest good, our best creative opportunities, and our most valuable connections.

Acknowledging intuition as natural and placing importance on it are two fundamental decisions necessary to jump-start your super sense back into action. It's the equivalent of turning on your inner GPS. But it is the third decision that is the most life-changing. That is to listen to your intuition and follow it without hesitation when it does communicate. This is the most empowering and practical decision you can make today.

Understanding Your Intuition

Intuition is guidance that comes from your authentic Self, your Spirit (as opposed to your limited ego Self). Your Spirit does not communicate to you through thoughts or words. Instead, it transmits information energetically through your body, like your other senses do. You don't think intuition. You feel it. And I don't mean "feel" as in feeling an emotion. I mean sensing subtle energetic vibrations or signals that convey a more accurate understanding of what is happening in your life than meets the eye or is evident now. Intuition works like energetic traffic signals, such as red, yellow, and green, or like merge, caution, and stop signs, depending on the message. Your Spirit communicates like a satellite GPS, revealing the road ahead by sending advance warnings and helpful directions as you go. Once you accept that you have this super sense, you automatically seek out its signals to guide you.

Like road signs, your intuition is easy to miss if your inner GPS is turned off or if you aren't paying attention, are distracted, or tune it out. If this is the case, you waste time, end up where you don't want to be, get turned around, veer off course, or become lost entirely. Intuition helps you avoid this trouble and quickly shows you how to get where you want to go in the safest, most direct way possible. It also points out the scenic route you might otherwise not notice because you didn't even know it existed and connects you with great traveling life companions. Intuition is a reliable compass, constantly guiding you to safety and flow and away from unwanted disturbance and trouble. And it does so in a subtle, gentle, whispering way.

My client Adam was on his way to meet some friends for a drink after watching the Rockies play their seasonal weekly baseball game in lower downtown Denver, Colorado, a few summers ago. He drove to the bar where they usually gathered and began looking for a parking space, but for some reason, his super sense nudged him to park a little farther away than usual and walk. So Adam followed his intuitive nudge and strolled over without giving it much thought. When he approached the bar, Adam noticed flashing lights, several cop cars, and policemen trying to contain a crowd. Wondering what was going on, he asked a bystander what had happened. The guy explained that a gang of about 20 teenage boys looking for trouble appeared out of nowhere, swarmed a group of people on the street, and beat and robbed them. Panicked, Adam muscled forward, only to see two of his best friends on the ground. Unfortunately, they had arrived at the wrong place and time, got caught in the melee, and were seriously hurt. Long story short, his friends were injured and robbed but fortunately survived.

By following his intuition and delaying his arrival at the bar by only minutes, Adam spared himself the ambush. It was no big deal at the time, but ultimately this little intuitive decision saved him from the fate of his friends. That's how intuition works. Like a whisper, it alerts you to pitfalls and disturbances between where you are and where you want to go and redirects you, if necessary, to smoother, safer energy and away from trouble. Your part is to pay attention and trust these nudges instead of questioning or ignoring them.

Today's Jump Start

Reclaim your missing piece, your intuition, and recognize it for the natural super sense that it is. Of course, you've already started doing this, or you wouldn't be reading this book, but still, bad habits die hard.

Answer the following:

- Do you fully accept that your intuition is a natural super sense, or do you continue to question or doubt whether this is true?

- Do you trust what your super sense feels or receives, or do you dismiss it?

- Are you presently aware of any intuitive signals? What are they?

Fully accepting your super-intuitive sense is the first step to using it. So reclaim your missing piece today by jump-starting your intuition back into action.

DAY 2

Follow Your Heart

Intuition follows the heart. It communicates most strongly about the things that matter most to us. For example, mothers often have keen intuition regarding their children's safety and well-being. People who work in finance have a super sense about investing. Fiction writers often receive intuitive "downloads," in which entire stories and characters drop into their awareness from out of nowhere. The same goes for other types of artists as well. Musicians intuitively hear the music they eventually score. Painters see visions that end up on the canvas. Some doctors can intuitively sense what is wrong with their patients before the tests return. Scientists who follow their instincts and hunches end up making huge breakthroughs. Builders can often immediately sense whether the ground under their feet is solid enough to build on before a single test is taken. The professional athlete turns his body toward the ball before his eyes see where it is going. Detectives follow their hunches when tracking crimes. As you can see, our super sense follows our passion.

As another example, I've personally written 30 books, all of which were inspired, even created, by spontaneous, intuitive downloads. Each time I begin writing a book, intuitive guidance immediately starts to flow once I settle in and get out of my head. I've never written a book proposal and wouldn't know how to. I love writing as much as I do because my books nearly write themselves.

Both of my daughters love to cook. When either of them enters a kitchen, their intuition and creativity kick right in, often in surprising ways. Once, when my daughter Sabrina was 10 years old, she announced to her class that she knew how to make sushi, even though she had never made sushi in her life. We rarely even ate sushi, for that matter, so this pronouncement came out of nowhere. Impressed, the teacher and her classmates invited her to demonstrate her culinary skills the next day.

When her father picked her up from school that afternoon, Sabrina calmly told him they had to go to a Japanese food market to buy supplies for making maki rolls. Being her father, he knew he had no choice but to say yes, and off they went in search of one.

With supplies in hand, Sabrina confidently walked into class the following day and, to the amazement of all, successfully made avocado maki rolls for everyone for lunch. That night I asked her how she did it. She simply shrugged and said, "I don't know. I just knew how."

That just demonstrates how much our intuition can offer (that is, if we don't block it or allow others to interfere with or block it either). Because it taps into the quantum field, our intuition can access much more information than our outer senses. It can guide us in extraordinary ways if we follow our heart, pursue what we love, and trust our sixth sense step-by-step as we go. Sabrina discovered this when making sushi that school day.

Intuition Helps You Create

I have a client named Aimee who loves redesigning old clothing into fresh, cool, modern outfits, an interest she picked up in middle school. Throughout high school, in pursuit of her passion, Aimee would follow her intuition to various resale shops around town, where she regularly discovered fabulous cast-off clothing made with sumptuous fabrics that she could never afford to buy new. The people who worked at these shops quickly came to know Aimee and marveled at her timing when finding the best vintage gems among the junk. Minutes after a great vintage dress or suit would be placed on the floor for sale, Aimee would show up, almost like clockwork. "You have great luck around here, Aimee," said one saleswoman at the local Salvation Army store Aimee popped in to occasionally. "I swear, the minute something fabulous shows up at the back door, you arrive at the front."

Aimee went on to design school after high school, and to this day, she scours vintage resale shops across the country and world looking for bargains that she turns into fantastic outfits. She is so successful that her designs draw people from all over to her shop, even celebrities.

"Without my super sense for vintage clothing, I'd be out of business," Aimee said at our last session. "It's the secret to my success. It leads me to find fabrics and clothing that simply aren't made anymore. I feel like a detective in search of the next great treasure!"

Lying behind what you love is your intuition, ready to guide you in how to bring what you love into your life. It's time to make that connection.

Today's Jump Start

Take your time contemplating the following questions:

- What is fun for you? What do you love to create?

- What and whom do you care about the most?

- What captures your imagination and heart?

Think about your answers throughout the day. Some interests might spring immediately to mind, and if so, notice how your intuition already helps. Other areas of curiosity and devotion may initially escape your mind but will pop up afterward. Now or later, notice how your intuition is right there, helping you succeed.

For example, I love more than just writing. I also love my family, my house, traveling, great restaurants, shopping, apartment hunting, making new friends, creating videos, watching foreign films, interior design, and fashion. And that is just off the top of my head.

My intuition helps me in all these areas. So much so, in fact, that I am often declared one of the luckiest people anyone knows. You can also be "lucky" by acknowledging what you love and letting your intuition get in on the game.

DAY 3

Start with
Common Sense

Your super sense detects vibrational waves of energy that arise from several places, some from inside your body and some from the world around you. These energetic broadcasts are primarily received in your heart and gut. Others are felt in the back of your head, in your arms, neck, and throat, up your spine, and some can even ring in your ears. We subconsciously receive intuitive waves of information more than we realize, as revealed by our expressions.

For example, intuitive vibrations traveling to and through our gut earn the phrase "gut feeling." Ones that travel up our spine give us "a chill." Intuitive vibrations travel through the hairs on the back of our necks and make them stand up. When we hear something energetically incongruent or untruthful, we'll say it doesn't "ring true." Intuitive waves of information can also affect our vision, hence the expressions "I just can't see that" or "I see what you mean." We even say, "That leaves a bad taste in my mouth" or "I smell a rat" when something does not intuitively resonate or feels untrue or unsafe. In all cases, we receive energetic communications in our bodies first before we try to decipher them with our brains. Therefore, it only stands to reason that the better condition your body is in, the better you can sense these valuable yet subtle intuitive messages trying to get your attention.

Your body needs care and maintenance to be a good receiver. It doesn't take much to recognize, for example, that when you're tired, hungry, or stressed, your body's bandwidth contracts and your intuition dims. When your body is well fed and relaxed, has enough water, and isn't besieged with stress, on the other hand, it tunes in much better to the energy around you and more intuitive messages come across. The more consistently well maintained and cared for your body is, the better your super sense will function.

Start with a Basic Check-In

How well do you care for your body? Do you eat well, or are you careless about what you eat? If you eat well, you know this sharpens your mind and turns your intuitive receiver on. Conversely, fatigue and brain fog set in if you don't eat well, and you tune out and can even pass out. If you want to tune in, it's best to steer clear of junk food, heavy or greasy food, and anything else that depletes your energy. Especially sugar. In fact, nothing kicks intuition offline faster than a blood-sugar nosedive after eating too many donuts or cookies on the run.

Smarter still, notice which foods best support your body and eat them. Stock up on fresh foods, such as fruits, veggies, and grains, and prepare them in advance so they're ready to grab and go and you don't get tempted by overprocessed options. Notice how much better you feel and how more intuitively aware you are when you eat healthy food.

When my client Natalie recognized how gluten gave her migraines and red wine made her depressed and angry, she stopped consuming both. Within days of these changes, her super sense lit up and guided her on more ways to improve her health and ease her depression, which she had suffered for years. Following her newly activated inner guidance, Natalie began a massive overhaul of her diet. In addition to avoiding gluten and alcohol, she cut out refined sugar, and in three months, she was off antidepressants for the first time in ten years. Now, I'm by no means saying diet cures depression; it just happened to work for Natalie. In retrospect, she said, "I knew my diet contributed to how badly I felt. Listening to my inner guidance, I'm now seeing a somatic therapist, as well and changing my career path. Thanks to my intuition, I've made many changes, but it started with my diet."

Preparing healthy food often means cooking for yourself, but this doesn't have to be a complicated or time-consuming chore either. In fact, cooking can be relaxing. My oldest daughter, Sonia, loves to prepare fresh vegetable soup while listening to her favorite podcasts as she unwinds after a long workday.

To sharpen your wits and jump-start your super sense, plan at least one balanced, fresh meal a day, and make it or have someone make it for you. There is such increased awareness about the importance of healthy food today that healthy options are available on most take-out apps, in case you aren't a cook or don't have time to cook.

What we drink affects intuition as well. Dehydration shrinks awareness, and water is the cure. Though many factors affect how much water is needed in a day, a common goal to follow is to drink around six to eight glasses of water daily to hydrate properly. How much are you drinking? Coffee doesn't count. If anything, coffee and sugary drinks cause more dehydration, even if they are liquid. Alcohol dehydrates you the most, plus it shuts your intuition down by altering your perception and dulling your awareness.

Apply common sense to your self-care and body maintenance if you want to awaken your intuition; you will feel better all the way around. Skip that fourth cup of coffee, pass on the third cocktail, and drink more water instead. You will be surprised at how much more intuitive you become when your physical body is recharged with what it needs to feel good and function well.

Besides food and water, sleep is also an intuition basic, so getting a good night's sleep should also become a top priority. Start by going to bed earlier. To set yourself up for success, turn off the news, hide your phone, get the best pillow, and take a warm, relaxing bath before calling it a night. Listen to your favorite calming music in the tub, such as Baroque piano music by Pachelbel, Telemann, or Vivaldi, all easily found on Spotify. You can enhance the calming mood by turning off the overhead lights and basking in the glow of a scented lavender candle while you soak. Add some Epsom salts to the water to unwind your muscles, too. This also clears the aura and relaxes the brain.

Once in bed, focus on your breathing with your eyes closed. Imagine breathing in healing energy and breathing out everything else. Using your imagination, breathe into your heart and out through your belly. Imagine melting into the bed as you settle down. If you struggle to fall asleep, focus on rest and relaxation instead of trying to force sleep. Your body can restore itself if you let go.

During the day, create an inner space to take "psychic breathers." Don't schedule every moment; leave some free time to recharge. Then make sure you keep those appointments with yourself. Be sensitive to your body's signals and respond instead of ignoring them—for example, go to the bathroom when you need to instead of postponing it until you finish a project. Stretch when your back hurts instead of staying hunched over for hours. Move your body, and it will sharpen your attention.

Finally, addictions, especially to drugs and alcohol, scramble your super sense and undermine your good intentions. Leave behind the swamp of self-sabotaging behavior as you reach for higher ground. Before you go one step further, be honest and admit if you need help with addictions. If you drink too much alcohol or experience negative effects from drinking any amount of alcohol, it's time to stop. The same goes for smoking marijuana, taking drugs, overeating, gambling, or overloading your body with anything that diminishes your ability to tune in and be aware. Even an addiction to shopping can dull your senses, so be honest, get sober, and seek advice and support if necessary.

If your body has the support it needs, it naturally becomes an excellent intuitive receiver. When well cared for, it regularly broadcasts and receives messages that will keep you alive, well, and in the flow. So tune up and tune in. It could even save your life.

Today's Jump Start

Today, assess your body's overall well-being. Is it time for an overhaul? Do you need a major tune-up or just a little more water? This day is about connecting what you put into your body with how it affects your intuition. Identify a few ways in which you can better support your body so it works well as an intuitive receiver. Start with one or two minor changes or improvements, such as having a protein shake for breakfast instead of a donut and drinking water instead of soft drinks or more coffee during the day, and go from there. The key is to recognize what supports your body and what doesn't and then make one or two smart changes that will help you both feel better and be more aware.

DAY 4

Get Grounded

To best tune in to our intuition, it is helpful to be calm and grounded. This is because when we are grounded, we are in a more relaxed, clear, receptive state, which enables us to perceive subtle energy (which intuition is) that we would otherwise miss. However, it is far more challenging to tune in to inner guidance when we are ungrounded because, when ungrounded, we are in a state of emergency, also known as "fight-or-flight." This agitated, reactive state tunes out our heart and inner voice and propels us a million miles away from helpful guidance. In fact, we can't hear much of anything when we're ungrounded because our fears are screaming too loud.

Unfortunately, this is when we need our super sense to guide us the most. We've all had those moments—facing drama at work, navigating a challenging situation or an angry person at home, or when we're stuck in traffic and on the verge of missing our flight with no backup plan. Sadly, our intuition goes up in smoke in these ungrounded moments, and our fears consume us. But this doesn't have to occur if we can recognize when we become ungrounded, what causes it, and what fixes it and, most important, if we can reground ourselves as quickly as possible.

How Do You Know If You Are Ungrounded?

Let's start by recognizing when you are ungrounded. When you're ungrounded, you may emotionally feel:

- Stressed

- Reactive

- Anxious

- Distracted

- Fearful

- Angry

- Defensive

- Overwhelmed

- Flooded

- Ambivalent

- Forgetful

- Impatient

- Disinterested

- Restless

- Moody

- Threatened or unsafe

- Like your circuits are blowing

When ungrounded, you may also physically feel:

- Weak

- Shaky

- Teary

- Exhausted

- Brain-fogged

- Agitated

- Checked out

- Panicky

- Shortness of breath or that you're breathing shallowly

You may even physically check out or run away from your situation if ungrounded enough. It's the classic fight-or-flight state we all know so well.

Moreover, since we are energetically responsive beings, a highly ungrounded person can also destabilize other people's energy. This often triggers a domino effect of anxiety, causing an avalanche of reactive emotions in those nearby. Think of a typical family fight on vacation where you can't find your hotel, or everyone is hungry and there's no food to be found at a late hour, causing a group meltdown and an outburst of angry, blaming words erupting in the car.

As we know, life today is stressful, and anxiety is contagious. Just as feeling ungrounded as an individual can lead us to feel jittery, on edge, and unable to think clearly, feeling ungrounded as a society can lead people down rabbit holes of paranoid groupthink and conspiracy. When we're ungrounded, we lose our sense of perspective and judgment, and it becomes difficult to access our intuition and receive the inner guidance we need.

My newly married client Denise and her husband, Jake, recently began renovating an old Victorian home in Chicago, their first real estate purchase. Shortly into the project, they found the scope of what they took on far more massive, expensive, overwhelming, and stressful than they could ever have imagined. This was hugely ungrounding to both.

Their chaotic living space, the brain-searing noise of construction, and the unexpected hemorrhaging costs of their project left Denise and Jake extraordinarily agitated and overwhelmed. Not realizing they were so ungrounded, they tried to regain control and solid ground by fighting with the contractors and their co-workers but mainly with each other. Before they knew it, they were separated and threatened each other with divorce.

When Denise came for an intuitive reading with me during this difficult time, she said, "I am so confused. When we bought this house, my intuition was confident it was the right thing for us. I knew it would be stressful, but not to this level. However, ever since we moved in and started the renovation, I fear I've made the biggest mistake of my life. I cannot stand the mess, the noise, the cost, and most of all, Jake. I get so furious with him for being so negative and reactive that I want to kick him out. How could my intuition be so wrong?"

I understood how Denise felt. The situation she and Jake were in was incredibly ungrounding, which does bring out the worst in anyone. Instead of helping each other get regrounded and find their way back to the center, they projected all their anxiety onto each other and split farther apart.

I assured Denise that her intuition did not mislead her into buying this house. It was a great buy, and she and Jake would love it in time, but only if they got grounded and stopped going after one another during this period. I reminded her it wouldn't last forever, but they needed to reset to make it through.

Once she understood the toll being so ungrounded was taking on them, Denise asked Jake to enroll in a boxing class with her to discharge their intense emotions and keep them from attacking one another. It worked. Last I heard, they survived the renovation and are still taking boxing classes.

What Ungrounds You?

Many things can unground us, especially in the anxiety-provoking topsy-turvy world we live in today. Being ungrounded happens when you lose touch with a solid sense of security in your body, home, job, friendships, and even the earth, with climate change, causing so much upheaval.

Being ungrounded first occurs when your body does not get what it needs to function correctly. You can quickly get ungrounded if you are tired, hungry, or thirsty, so I focused on that topic yesterday.

External influences can also unground you. Many people are unaware of this, but something as simple as loud, dissonant, and disturbing noise can leave you feeling profoundly ungrounded, especially if you are empathic or highly sensitive or grew up in a family with much yelling and fighting.

Change, even positive change, in your environment or routine can also be highly ungrounding. Humans feel safest when life is predictable; when that disappears, we feel threatened, another sign of feeling ungrounded. Predictable circumstances leave us feeling rooted in our lives. They give us a sense of safety and belonging. Change to that predictable flow often causes us to feel unsafe and uncertain, as it did with Denise and Jake.

Situations and people that scare you unground you. Financial troubles, an untrustworthy partner, a sudden illness, or even a new love affair can unground you because you may feel out of control. We are sensitive creatures and get easily ungrounded if we aren't aware. It happens every day. And, of course, any dangerous situation or situation in which you feel your personal boundaries being violated, from pickpocketing to assault, can be profoundly traumatic and destabilizing.

Everyday Things That Unground Us:

- Poor boundaries

- Change

- Overcommitting

- Arguing

- Power struggles

- Violence

- Being around a withholding or aggressive person

- Stonewalling

- Being bullied

- Being attacked

- Feeling vulnerable

- Feeling isolated

- Money troubles or unexpected bills

In other words, almost anything in life can unground you, making it necessary for you to have the tools to get grounded again as fast as possible. Only then can you stay tuned in to your intuition and follow your super sense back to solid ground.

Today's Jump Start

Get grounded. Start with taking a personal time-out of five minutes at least once today. Sit by yourself and ask that no one disturb you. Sitting for five minutes can reregulate your nervous system, relax your emotions, and reconnect you to the earth. You will feel the difference. Better yet, do it outside, on a park bench or somewhere else with a connection to nature. This will remind you of how being grounded feels. Then it will be easier to recognize when you are ungrounded and quickly reset in the future.

Fortunately, getting grounded is not difficult. It mostly takes awareness and a few practical adjustments to reconnect. The first step is to breathe. This sounds obvious, but we hold our breath because we are afraid when we're ungrounded. This puts us in a state of fight, flight, or freeze. Breathing fuels our brains with oxygen, which helps us focus and centers us back in our bodies again.

Start by sitting in a chair with both feet on the floor and your back straight. Next, breathe slowly in through your nose, then exhale out of your mouth, like you're blowing out candles through a straw, two or three times. This breathing technique releases the adrenaline that floods into your system when ungrounded and helps you calm down and reset.

Once you feel calmer, resume normal breathing. As you breathe, place one hand on your chest and the other on your belly. Imagine planting your feet into the ground, and if possible, envision them as having roots, digging deep into the earth. Close your eyes and, using your imagination, breathe up from your feet and into your belly. Imagine exhaling out of your heart, releasing your stress back to the Universe as you do.

Do this at least 10 times or more if time affords.

Once you feel grounded and relaxed, turn your attention to your intuition and ask your super sense what to do next. Then answer out loud, letting your inner guidance speak.

Here are some other ways to quickly reground as well. Because so much of our grounding is centered in our physical body and nervous system, returning to the self-care addressed yesterday works best to reground.

Try:

- Eating some nuts or protein in the morning

- Drinking a glass of room-temperature water six to eight times a day

- Watching a funny television program

- Listening to music

- Taking time alone

- Taking a walk

- Stopping whatever you are doing

- Dancing

- Cooking

- Drawing

- Playing an instrument

- Working in the garden

- Folding your laundry

- Laughing

- Exercising

- Telling yourself everything is okay or will soon be

- If extremely ungrounded, getting into the shower and screaming

DAY 5

Meet the Messenger

The most immediate way to tune in to your intuition is by listening to the direct energetic feedback of your physical body. Your mind tends to tune in to your ego, which filters out and distorts information, believes what isn't necessarily true, and can even convince you to betray yourself or worse. On the other hand, your body listens to your Spirit, which honestly and accurately reflects how energy impacts you on a vibrational level and guides you toward safety and optimum outcomes. Your super sense communicates via subtle physical signals, such as aches, pains, flutters, ripples, tightness, fatigue, or even sickness, all to keep you safe and aligned with your authentic Self. Of course, these intuitive signals vary depending on what they are trying to tell you.

Thankfully your body is an honest, straightforward, intuitive messenger. If you're on the right track, doing what supports your soul and Spirit, you will feel more at ease, full of life, relaxed, peaceful, and in the flow. Your heart will open and beat steadily. Your energy will increase, and you'll be relatively free from stress. If, on the other hand, you're making choices that compromise or ignore your inner guidance, or if you find yourself in dissonant energetic situations or with people who threaten or disrupt your well-being, your heart will pound, your stress will rise, your hypervigilance will kick in, sleep may be harder to come by, and your body may even hurt.

If you ignore these physical signals long enough, your body will increase the volume and try harder to get your attention. These louder signals result in greater tension, irritability, insomnia, reactivity, anxiety, or minor to more significant physical disturbances. And if you ignore your body's signs completely, a "red alert" siren may sound in the way of a more significant physical disorder, and there's a chance that you could become ill or depressed.

Body Language

Fortunately, your body's signals are easy enough to read. After that, it's mostly a matter of deduction. For example, problems with your legs or feet usually reflect feeling uncertain about where you're going in life or feeling ungrounded, stuck, or insecure about being sufficiently self-reliant and able to stand on your own two feet.

My client Laura started feeling pins and needles in her feet and lower legs. She also felt a strange numbness in them, which distracted her. She went to a doctor who diagnosed her with inexplicable and incurable neuropathy and told her there was not much she could do about it. Her super sense told her their prognosis was wrong. Her first stop was a naturopath who gave her supplements, B vitamins, and a stretching protocol to relieve her symptoms. This all helped. Then he asked her what she thought her feet were telling her that she might be ignoring. She immediately knew the answer. Not having ever said so before, she admitted she had wanted to move away from Detroit, where she had been living unhappily with her alcoholic boyfriend of 10 years, and return to her beloved friends and family on the East Coast.

She intuitively knew that the tingles in her feet were simply her body's signaling that it was time to let go and move on. Her feet fell asleep, resigned to a life that was all wrong for her, and she needed to wake them up. With this nerve-racking condition, Laura was forced to stop ignoring her guidance and left just before Christmas. She hasn't regretted it since. The neuropathy subsided slowly over the next few years, but she knew it would have become far worse had she ignored her body's prompts to get going.

Gastrointestinal difficulties, irritable bowels, reflux, and other digestive troubles can signal that you feel overwhelmed, emotionally undernourished, or that you're unable to digest life or "stomach" certain conditions. My client Roxanne, an only child of highly wealthy parents, suffered from IBS and diarrhea for years. After eliminating every dietary and medical reason possible, one day, just before going to sleep, she asked her body why this was happening. She was tired of suffering. Ten minutes later, she was flooded with a desire to stop depending on her parents and grow up. She loved cooking healthy foods and desserts and had long wanted to start an online blog to share her recipes with others who suffered the same digestive challenges. She was sick of being lazy and unchallenged and felt guilty about living such a luxurious life without using her creativity in a purposeful way. Underneath her illness, Roxanne was bored and disappointed that she didn't challenge herself more, making her feel sick.

Her super sense told her that her nonstop digestive illnesses were her ego's way of punishing her for being so passive and reliant. The minute she admitted this, her stomach relaxed.

The next day she started an Instagram channel devoted to creating simple, healthy, gluten-, dairy-, and sugar-free desserts. It took a while, but eventually Roxanne gained a respectable following and even started to make money by selling her delicious recipes in an online cookbook. Once she decided to take responsibility for herself and do something she loved, her chronic IBS subsided and eventually went away altogether.

Heart concerns are often associated with feeling disconnected from your emotions or may reflect challenges around giving and/or receiving love. At the same time, neck and throat issues may relate to difficulty speaking up or out, being heard, or listening to the world with an open mind and heart. Difficulties with your eyes often indicate problems with perception, outlook, and point of view, such as not wanting to see or being afraid of seeing what's ahead.

This is, of course, a highly simplified version of how the Spirit communicates with the body—and it's certainly not intended in any way as a substitute for seeking expert help whenever you have physical issues. It is only to say our bodies communicate what our minds can ignore, bury, deny, tune out, or just plain miss. Your body is your best friend and an honest messenger. Therefore, taking care of your body should include listening to its energetic signals. More and more doctors recognize this mind–body–spirit connection to health and ask their patients about their intuition to help treat them. Our bodies are highly sophisticated and complex. Therefore, we need to love them, listen to them, and give them all the support they need to be healthy.

When You've Abandoned Ship

Sadly, many people have suffered physical, emotional (especially through body-shaming), and/or sexual abuse. One way they've survived such horrific violations is to become completely numb to their bodies. This strategy works well until you can get to safe and supportive healers who can assist in your recovery. However, it is not a good long-term or a lifelong approach because when you numb yourself, you become even more vulnerable to violation.

If you've suffered violence or abuse or struggle to feel comfortable in your body, please know you can heal. Some effective ways to do this are practicing gentle yoga, learning to do breath work, and seeing a practitioner who works with a therapy called EMDR (eye movement desensitization and reprocessing). One of the best books in the world for healing from past physical abuse and body shame that elaborates on the above suggestions is *The Body Keeps the Score* by Dr. Bessel van der Kolk. The book is easy to read and offers profound healing guidance for anyone who is numb to their body or stuck in body trauma. Indeed, it is worthwhile reading for everyone.

Today's Jump Start

Be kind to your body today. It is your best friend and a powerful, honest, loving messenger to be cared for and loved by you. For starters, do not criticize your body at all. If you are in the habit of rejecting any part of your body, feeling it is unacceptable somehow, apologize. For example, if you routinely lament your weight, body size, hair or lack thereof, the size of your feet, the state of your skin, or any other aspect of your physical Self, stop and say, "I'm sorry, body. I love you. Please forgive me. Thank you for being the perfect vessel for my Spirit in this life." Or simply say, "I'm sorry. I love and appreciate you."

On the other hand, you can compliment your body, and I encourage you to do this regularly. For example, say, with enthusiasm, "I love my hair." "I love my bright smile and my gorgeous energy." "I am so grateful for my physical health and strength." "I am beautiful, inside and out." Appreciative statements like these reestablish and strengthen the intuitive conversation between your body and mind because we listen more closely to what we love and value.

Next, ask if there is anything your body is trying to tell you, then answer out loud. Stay out of your head, and don't let your logical brain interfere with this conversation. Instead, listen to what your body is saying and trust your intuitive interpretation. If something feels off, acknowledge it. The same goes for things that feel positive and encouraging. Be curious and open to any underlying messages. Observe with interest and ask your body what, if anything, is wrong. Your body will tell you what and why if you want to know.

It doesn't take a mystic to read and understand your body's messages—after all, it's your body. The more you pay attention to and attempt to understand your body's signals, the more precisely you will be able to interpret the intuitive guidance it provides.

DAY 6

Meditate

One of the best ways to tune in to your intuition is to meditate. Meditation helps awaken your super sense in several ways. First, it quiets your mind and allows you to tune in to the more subtle insights and feelings that thinking and strong emotions can drown out. Meditation is simply the daily practice of quieting the mind and relaxing. It doesn't stop us from thinking or feeling. Instead, it helps us detach from our thoughts and eases our reactivity to the world, inside and out.

Meditation reminds us to breathe, which is a great relief, especially for those who are often rushing around, trying to manage more than feels comfortable, and having difficulty keeping up with demands. In those cases, we may find ourselves breathing shallowly, holding our breath with our hearts racing, and in a state of constant hypervigilance, none of which are good for our health—mental or physical. If this is the case, meditation becomes our medication. Finally, it reminds us that we are not the thoughts that race through our minds, many of which are harmful, fearful, or full of anxiety and dread. Instead, meditation encourages us to step back and gently observe our thoughts and feelings as though they were no more than cars passing on the road. Meditating teaches us to let them go by rather than chase after them.

Meditation creates more open space in our heads and more room in our bodies and gives us access to our inner voice. It grounds us and allows us to breathe, relax, regroup, calm down, shift from fight-or-flight reactivity to observation and objectivity, and move toward more conscious, intuitively guided responses.

Meditation helps us make better choices in our lives. It softens our hearts, opens our minds, eases our stress, and gets the mental "tigers" off our tails that bully and push us around and leave us feeling defensive and under siege. Meditation is the most immediate way to connect to inner guidance. It helps us tune in to our Higher Self, angels, guides, and entire Divine support system and invites us to feel reassured by the loving caress of the Universe every day.

One of the most compelling reasons to meditate is that it helps you check in with your intuition before acting. With practice, it keeps you from acting on impulse, being too reactive to what's happening around you, or being controlled by the fears inside you, which can lead you to make automatic and unproductive decisions or veer off track. Instead, it lets you calmly access your intuition about what is best for you before acting.

For example, my client Nora, a customer service agent for a large department store, struggled to keep her callers happy, as they usually contacted the store feeling agitated, angry, and ready for a fight. Most days she went home feeling exhausted, overwhelmed, and emotionally beat up by the frustrated people who lashed out at her on the phone with their disappointments and upsets, failing to recognize she was only trying to help.

Still, she loved her job and managed to keep her spirits up and do her best until an ambitious new manager showed up. Eager to improve their store's overall customer service ratings, the new boss started monitoring all the customer service agents at the store, including Nora, and began to regularly criticize them for not doing enough (according to her). She notably seized upon Nora, accusing her of not quickly resolving issues with clients or being a productive enough team member to raise the store's rating. She further accused Nora of having a bad attitude and being hard to communicate with, as Nora often sat silent after being berated by her boss, stunned by accusations that had never been leveled at her before. If anything, Nora prided herself on how well she listened to clients and helped them. Unfortunately, it was her new boss who wasn't attentive, communicative, or helpful.

Day after day, Nora began to feel increasingly attacked and defensive under this ceaseless assault. Finally, one day, after dealing with a nonstop barrage of outraged clients and her oppressive boss, Nora lost her temper and screamed at her boss to get off her back.

That didn't go over well, and Nora was given a warning by HR and told she needed to attend a communication-improvement course to keep her job. Nora called me, beside herself. She was outraged, angry, and scared and didn't know how to turn the situation around, even though she knew she must. She was not free to lash out as she had and needed to get a grip on her emotions despite the constant provocation and criticism she was now experiencing on top of the already incredibly stressful demands of the job. "I don't want to lose my job," she cried, "but I just can't stand my boss and don't know what to do."

I encouraged Nora to meditate to relieve her stress, ease her reactivity, and find her way to inner guidance. I clarified that while meditating would not replace self-control, it would enhance her ability to exercise it and be guided on what to do next. Desperate, she agreed. Nora began slowly, using a simple four-breath technique to help herself calm down. I encouraged her to do this meditation every morning and when challenged by people or situations during the day at work. Relieved to have something to grab on to, she agreed to try it.

Several weeks later, she called to tell me that she had decided to quit her job. In fact, she was determined to do so, even though she didn't have another job to go to. But while meditating, she suddenly had a strong intuition to hang in there. She followed her guidance and decided to stay a little longer even though she was totally fed up. Three insufferable days later, her boss's superior called her into the office. Oh no, she thought. This is it. I'm going to get sacked. Instead, she was informed that her awful boss had been let go. She was offered the now-vacant position.

"Had I not started meditating," she shared, "I would be a jobless, resentful mess. Instead, I am calmer than ever, can deal with more stress, feel connected to my inner guidance like never before, and I got a promotion!"

Today's Jump Start

Try this "I AM calm" meditation. Start the day with the same short meditation I taught Nora:

Sit quietly in a chair or upright in your bed with your back straight and eyes open. Place one hand on your heart and one on your belly. Look around the room and reassure yourself you are safe. When you feel comfortable, gently close your eyes and fully exhale. Then breathe into the hand on your heart to the count of four. Hold to the count of four. Next, breathe out of the hand on your belly to the count of four. Hold again to the count of four. Repeat.

As you breathe in, say to yourself, "I am calm." As you breathe out, repeat this statement. Breathe in, "I am calm." Breathe out, "I am calm." Continue until you feel calm. Five to 10 minutes of meditation is enough to jump-start your super sense.

DAY 7

Be Mindful

In addition to meditating, being mindful is a tremendously beneficial skill to develop to awaken your intuition. It's also a beautiful practice that can truly transform your life. Mindfulness means consciously bringing your full attention to the present moment and embracing it with open arms, without resistance or judgment. Being mindful means welcoming whatever thoughts, feelings, or circumstances arise as you move through your day with a relaxed response.

Mindfulness means getting out of your head and paying attention to the here and now. This ideally allows you to experience the richness of life and the beauty in every single moment instead of being swept away by the constant noise and reactive joy-stealing chatter of your fearful emotions and distracting thoughts. Being mindful also means not jumping to conclusions and allowing your intuition to guide you instead of your ego.

How to Be More Mindful

Being mindful starts with paying attention to where you are right now. Mindfulness practice trains your mind to settle down, be quiet, and notice the world as it unfolds. It spares you the unnecessary emotional wear and tear that comes with resisting what is happening or the frustration of feeling you are missing out that comes with being preoccupied, rushed, and distracted—something all too common in our tech-dominated world.

Mindfulness creates the inner space and emotional bandwidth to respond to life intentionally rather than freak out over, fight against, or miss what is happening in the moment. It's the "stop and smell the flowers" invitation that is offered to us all.

Becoming mindful is easier than you think. It begins with the willingness to make being present a priority. Once you decide to become more mindful, the only other challenge is to remember to practice. One of the biggest reasons being mindful develops your intuition is that besides quieting the noise and distractions of everyday life and inviting you to turn inward, it creates the quiet needed for your intuitive inner voice to be heard. Being mindful calms your nervous system and amplifies your senses so you don't miss the subtle intuitive signals and clues that noisy mind chatter drowns out. Being mindful also invites your Higher Self, your Spirit, to lead you as you move through the day so you receive intuitive downloads more quickly and easily. In fact, mindfulness amplifies intuition. The more mindful you are, the quieter your internal environment gets and the more connected to your inner voice you become.

Marianne, a talented architect and rising star in Chicago, could barely stand her colleague June from the first day they were asked to work on a project together. Marianne found June arrogant, impatient, unimaginative, and critical of Marianne's ideas, which infuriated her. The tension between the two became so bad that Marianne asked to be transferred off the project and told her boss, whom she got along with well, why. But rather than being sympathetic and agreeing to her request, her boss told Marianne to stick it out until the project ended because they were doing such a great job together despite their differences. Not knowing how she could stand June for six more months until the project ended, Marianne came to me, looking for advice. I suggested to Marianne that she practice mindful listening with June, something she had never even heard of but was willing to try.

During their weekly project meeting the following Monday, Marianne applied some of the mindfulness tools I shared with her. Rather than roll her eyes and tune June out as Marianne usually did, she gave June her complete, unbiased, nonjudgmental attention and listened to what she had to say. When she listened mindfully, Marianne was impressed by how creative June was. To her surprise, Marianne also intuitively sensed that underneath June's obnoxious behavior, she felt somehow threatened by Marianne. This unexpected insight surprised Marianne and cooled her reactivity down considerably. In fact, once Marianne better understood June's behavior toward her, she wondered if her own adverse reaction to June had been a manifestation of her competitive streak and not about June at all.

Enlightened by these surprising back-to-back intuitive downloads, Marianne suddenly found it easier to acknowledge June's excellent ideas and even support them. When she did, the energy shifted between them. The undercurrent of toxic competition and negativity suddenly transformed to a more collaborative and cooperative flow. While Marianne could hardly say that she and June became best friends, mindful listening did allow Marianne to develop a newfound respect for June and enabled her to focus on the project and less on her emotions. Ultimately, the work was successfully completed, and both June and Marianne received professional recognition for a well-done job. Later, Marianne thanked me, citing how mindfulness helped her career take a huge leap forward. "I was so ready to jump ship," she said, laughing, convinced June was a terrible partner. "Being mindful revealed a more accurate picture of everything going on and helped me see how little was about June and how much was about me. I'll probably never work with June again, but hanging in there, like my intuition told me to, was the best thing to do for my career. Mindfulness is now something I practice to this day with everyone I work with."

Mindful listening involves being fully present and attentive to the person you're conversing with, with patience and without judgment or preconceived notions. It consists of setting your thoughts and opinions aside and allowing yourself to be genuinely available to what you are experiencing of another person now. While it's not easy, if you are willing to learn, it can transform your professional and personal relationships.

When mindfully listening, focus on the person's tone of voice, words, and body language. Notice how your intuition pipes in as you listen this way.

Mindfully listening to the environment is also helpful as you travel through your day. For example, my client Matthew told me he found himself on a crowded subway in New York City on his way to work one morning, squeezed between a man with a large backpack and a woman holding a screaming baby. The noise and the commotion were overwhelming, and his stress was rising fast, something he didn't need, as he had a big presentation to give that morning.

Choosing to be mindful, Matthew stopped fighting and resenting his circumstances and started focusing on his breath and the sensations in his body instead. After a few breaths, his mind quieted, and his tension eased, but his intuition suddenly urged him to get off at the next stop, even though this wasn't remotely close to work. Following this signal, Matthew quickly jumped off at the next station and walked the extra 10 blocks to work. As he did, he continued his mindful practice. He listened to the birds singing in the sky. He noticed the smell of fresh coffee wafting from the street vendor on the corner. He even noticed the sound of clicking shoes on the pavement as people like him scurried to work.

The walk calmed him down, for which he was grateful, and he arrived in both good spirits and plenty of time to make an excellent presentation. Later that afternoon, Matthew heard there was a significant delay on the line he had jumped off early that morning, and people were stranded, unable to get off the train for hours. Matthew's mindfulness spared his nervous system and saved his workday. That was all he needed to make it a regular practice.

Today's Jump Start

Today, practice these three easy ways to encourage a more mindful state of being.

First, pay attention to your breathing and how it feels as air flows in and out of your body. Concentrate on the sensation of the air flowing through your nostrils, into your upper chest and lower belly, and then out. As you inhale, feel the cool air entering your nostrils and filling your lungs, and as you exhale, feel your mind becoming calm and quiet. Breathe in the new; release the old. Following three or four rounds of this slow, mindful breathing, with eyes open, notice how much more aware you are and how much more inner space you suddenly have, making room for your intuition to be heard.

Second, practice eating mindfully. So many of us are on the run these days, doing far more than is healthy in a day, so we often either eat so fast, we don't taste our food, gulping it down as we race from one appointment to the next, or we don't eat at all, which strains the body, depletes our energy, and lowers our awareness. And so, of course, intuitive perception goes out the door.

Mindful eating simply means slowing down and tasting your food. Notice the texture, color, flavor, and aroma of each morsel you put in your mouth. Fight the urge to rush through this; instead, take your time chewing every bite you take. Pause between bites. Being mindful might feel like torture if you are not used to eating slowly, but hang in there. A mindful breakfast takes only a few more minutes than a mindless one and improves everything—body, mind, and intuition. It's worth the effort.

Third, practice listening mindfully. When you genuinely listen to others, you pick up on subtle clues that reveal emotions, intentions, and desires you might otherwise miss, fueling your intuition and decision-making. It improves understanding, forges connections, and elevates creativity.

The secret to mindfulness is to slow down and breathe deeply and often as you move through the day. The immediate benefit is not feeling rushed and pressured, allowing you to enjoy yourself far more.

Week 2
OWN IT

Last week you awakened your intuition superpower, recognized its unique signals in your body, and created the ideal conditions for getting your intuition to work magic in your life. This week we will continue this empowering, life-changing adventure by identifying and removing any self-sabotaging attitudes and behaviors that block your intuition and keep you in the dark. We will also develop practical skills and habits to access your intuition on demand.

DAY 8

Remove
the Roadblocks

If intuition is so natural and beneficial, why are people so reluctant to consult theirs today? The answer is that, unfortunately, we've been blocked in the past, often before we could recognize just how vital this natural super sense is. The three main roadblocks preventing us from using our intuition are religious training, scientific bias, and learned closed-mindedness.

The Religious Training Block

The first and most common block comes from our past religious training. Many of us have been raised to believe in a powerful authoritarian God and a religion suggesting that we are fundamentally flawed and not trustworthy enough to lead our own lives. This message further implies we must look to authoritative, patriarchal figures to guide us in life instead of listening to or trusting ourselves. These authoritarian figures are found at the heads of churches, temples, or mosques and the family.

At its most toxic and superstitious level, some ideologies even teach that inner guidance is the work of the "devil" or his "maleficent forces." However, this ridiculous perception is thankfully fading. Growing up Catholic, I experienced much of this patriarchal indoctrination firsthand. So much so that I felt it necessary to go underground with my super sense as early as the age of eight or nine because the nuns at school disapproved of my intuition. Maybe you've experienced some version of this as well. Sadly, many authorities still believe we must silence our inner voice and submit to outer spiritual authorities instead.

While we may not consciously adhere to these beliefs today, these old indoctrinations continue to float around in our subconscious minds, imprinted so deeply and early in our lives that they dim and distort our perceptions.

To clear this block, recognize that the true authority in life is your Spirit, which speaks to you through inner guidance. For example, when asked by a partner or friend where you would like to go to dinner, rather than automatically saying, "I don't care. Where would you like to go?" take a moment, check in with your intuition, and choose a place that feels appealing to you. If people around you aren't used to you expressing an opinion, they might push back and quickly dismiss your suggestion, so be prepared for this possibility. There's no need to fight or argue if your input is rejected. Simply say, "Well, that's my preference. You asked." Sharing a restaurant preference is no big deal, so there's no risk in letting others know what you feel. But it paves the way for sharing more significant feelings such as "I don't feel safe with so-and-so" and sticking to your instinct.

Both you and people around you will soon get used to having you listen to your inner voice and express it aloud, which may be different from the past. Begin easy and go from there. Practice asserting your personal truth daily in small ways, as opportunities present themselves, rather than being quiet or going along with something you do not feel in your heart. You have the right to reject belief systems that do not resonate with you. If you do, you will feel more authentic and aligned with your Spirit and inner guidance.

The Intellectual Block

The second most common block to listening to your natural super sense is the belief that intuition is not scientifically based and therefore not worth paying attention to. Anyone who believes this cites last century's science and hasn't checked in with today's current scientific updates. Science is not a closed book. It evolves over time.

For example, in the Middle Ages, scientists said the earth was flat. What yesterday's flat-earthers believed proved untrue in time and with more information and understanding of our planet. Scientists of the past also insisted that the sun rotated around the earth, and anyone who disagreed, like Copernicus, was jailed for challenging this belief. Today's science, thank goodness, and most notably quantum physics, recognizes that we are more than physical beings and have more than five senses to guide us. Scientists do not yet fully understand our spiritual nature or exactly how our intuitive super sense operates, but they are working on it. In time, I'm sure they will.

When people tell me they don't believe in intuition because it is not scientifically supported, I ask which science they are referring to. Usually, they can't say because they are simply parroting something poorly learned in middle school.

You may not personally have a scientific block, but you may be surrounded by others who do, which cramps your intuitive flow. I have a highly intuitive friend, Gordon, who regularly meets with four of his lifelong friends for a weekly coffee. All four are accomplished, successful businessmen and investors in their fifties, and all pride themselves on being science-based intellectuals. Not surprisingly, all four guys laugh out loud at Gordon when he shares anything he intuitively feels. Gordon loves his friends, so he doesn't take offense at this mockery, but he does think twice before sharing his super sense with them and occasionally wonders if he is indeed "nuts," as they suggest. He recently shook his head when sharing with me how confident his friends are that he is "looney" and how they never acknowledge when his intuition proves accurate, which they have also observed over the years. "I called the bank financial collapse months before it happened in 2023 during many morning coffees with these guys," he said, "but they refused to acknowledge this when it eventually did happen. They simply cannot validate my intuition because it isn't scientifically proven. It's too risky for them to think so independently."

Gordon is right about their hesitation. For many overly logically trained thinkers, following their intuitive super sense over what they've been trained to believe can feel risky, especially if they depend on other people's approval or the consensus for a sense of acceptance or self-worth. Gordon is willing to take the risk sometimes but not always. He listens to his intuition but thinks twice before fully believing it or telling his friends about it.

To overcome this block, realize you don't need other people's approval to listen to your inner guidance. If someone dismisses intuition as unscientific, just recognize them as today's "flat-earthers" and let it go. Don't even try to change their mind. You won't. Instead, smile and say, "Maybe I am crazy, but my intuition works for me." Then continue to follow your heart. Watching your life flourish by following your inner guidance will be far more effective in opening another's mind than arguing over its validity. Most flat-earthers eventually got on board in the past and will do the same when more scientific investigation and discovery validate our super sense. Have the patience and courage to follow your inner guidance instead of allowing others to silence you with their preconceived, closed-minded opinions.

The Closed-Minded Block

The third most common roadblock to using your super-intuitive sense is having a closed mind toward intuition because you grew up with closed-minded others and so carry on the habit. For example, I have a lovely hairdresser,

Isaac, in London, with whom I have become dear friends over the past few years. One day, as I got a haircut, he said, "I owe you an apology, Sonia." Surprised, as he had done nothing to offend me, I asked, "Why?"

"Because when you first told me you teach people to be more intuitive," he answered, "I immediately dismissed you as stupid, although, of course, I didn't say so. However," he continued, "because you are such a positive, energetic, confident person, which I don't encounter very often, I became curious and started following your Instagram and YouTube channels. To my surprise, I learned a lot that made sense to me. I realized I was being judgmental and closed-minded for no reason, so if anyone was stupid, it was me."

"Well, that's a little harsh." I smiled as he continued.

"Wait," he said. "There's more. Last week, I went to the gym, and my super sense, as you call it, gave me a bad feeling as I was putting my clothes in my locker. So much so that I considered changing lockers or even not working out. But because no one was around to confirm my suspicions, I pushed this feeling aside and went to work out anyway. When I returned, my locker had been broken, and my wallet and phone were gone. I immediately thought of you because I had been warned, yet I had ignored it. I really felt stupid then!"

Don't let an unfortunate event like the one Isaac suffered teach you the folly of dismissing your intuition out of habit. I playfully call people who ignore their super sense like Isaac did members of the "Woulda Coulda Shoulda Club of Missed Opportunity" because they would have been far better off if they had opened their minds and listened to their intuition. The antidote to a closed mind is to become curious and receptive to learning something new. My mom used to say, "Never assume what you know is all there is to know." This is so true.

Today's Jump Start

Today, start clearing the blocks. Start by identifying the roadblocks and blind spots hindering you and commit to removing them immediately. To do this, take a blank piece of paper and draw a line down the center. On the left side, at the top, write "Past Perceptions," and on the right, "Present Perceptions." First, consider your Religious Training Blocks.

On the left, write down all suggestions or influences you received directly or indirectly from your past religious training that suggested intuition was something bad to be feared, ignored, or distanced from. Did anyone in your family acknowledge intuition positively and naturally? Or did they treat it as unnatural or harmful? Who set the tone?

How did your religious training affect you? Write down everything from the past that comes up in this category. Next, on the right side of the paper, write down your spiritual perceptions today. Do you still hold on to any of these past religious feelings or beliefs? Do you feel any conflict between your past religious training and your present-day personal feelings, experiences, and spiritual beliefs? Do your family or friends hold different views from yours about intuition in general now? Does this present a conflict? Write down everything that feels like a block.

After you've reviewed your past religious blocks, now consider your Intellectual Roadblocks. On the left side of the paper, write down all past intellectual or scientific perceptions that influenced your outlook on intuition today. Did you come from a science-based background or a family of intellectuals where intuition was dismissed outright as "woo-woo," not evidence-based, or not "real"? Who held these perceptions? Parents? Extended family? Teachers? Friends? Write down all the people who held such perceptions and how they influenced you back then. Did you adopt these views? Or did you openly or secretly disagree? Were you unsure? Once you record these past perceptions, move to the right column and consider your updated, present-moment perceptions. To help you, Google how science perceives intuition today. Be curious but check in with your own experiences as well. No matter what "science" says, your inner guidance is an undeniable part of you, and your personal intuitive experiences count the most.

Finally, think about your Social and Other Unconscious Blocks. On the left side, write down any general negative or dismissive assumptions you or people close to you have carried about intuition up until now. Take your time, as this category reveals your super sense's most hidden and unconscious blocks. For example, do you or your friends and family joke about intuition, dismissing it as "coincidence"? Does anyone exaggerate and treat intuition as scary or bizarre? Do you instantly go to your head and look for logical explanations when you get an intuitive hit or hunch because that's what you've seen everyone in your life do in the past? Do you struggle to explain your intuition to yourself or others? Again, write down all learned dismissive behaviors and attitudes in the left column. Once you've completed this, go to the right side, and, this time, write down new attitudes, beliefs, and perceptions you'd like to adopt or presently have concerning your super sense today. These can be affirmations or statements of intent, such as "I don't need logical backup to trust my super sense" or "My intuition is my superpower, and I listen every time" or "I don't need an explanation or permission to trust my intuition because it is natural."

This exercise strengthens your intuition, brings it forward, out of the past and into the present empowering moment. Finally, before retiring tonight, reflect on what your intuition has been trying to communicate to you now that some of the obstacles are cleared away.

DAY 9

Name It,
Then Claim It

One of my psychic mentors, Charlie Goodman—a master metaphysician from England who taught me the psychic arts when I first began my apprenticeship with him at 12 years old—said, "Being aware of intuition is only one part of the process. Expressing it is the other. Only then does it begin to help you in life." Unfortunately, because so many people didn't grow up in families like mine where intuition was freely acknowledged, they often feel awkward or uncomfortable about expressing their inner awareness today. To a large degree, this may be simply because they don't have words that comfortably allow them to share their insights without self-consciousness. Thankfully, this can be quickly remedied: once you name it, you can claim it.

Express Your Vibes

In my family, intuition was so fundamental to our way of life that we had specific "code words" to acknowledge and express our higher wisdom. These terms were quite simple yet conveyed our intuition well. This code language made it easy for my siblings and me to share our intuitive feelings as naturally as talking about the weather. The fact that we even had particular words for our various intuitive flashes taught us that our inner perceptions were valid, worth noticing, and didn't need explaining.

The first of our code words were "vibes," which refers to the initial energetic sensation of intuition in the body. We divided intuition into categories: Good vibes were the happy, positive feelings evoked when we encountered people, places, ideas, synchronicities, and possibilities that were beneficial to us. Getting good vibes gave us a sense of protection and grace and indicated a "green light" or feeling that we should "go for it" when we had a decision to make. On the other hand, we also recognized bad vibes, which referred to all the uncomfortable feelings that cautioned us: "Keep away," "Don't do it," "Don't trust it," "Watch out," "Be careful," or "Stay on your toes!" They were instincts that alerted us that something should be avoided. Being empowered with these simple expressions made it easy to integrate my super sense into my life as just another everyday aspect of my awareness.

I've continued the tradition of "speaking vibes" with my daughters. I introduced them to the terms that were so familiar to me, and together we've invented others. For example, my daughter Sonia came up with "woolies" to describe how she feels when someone or something disrupts her inner harmony. It also refers to the conditions or people who irritate her—like wool on bare skin. When she says someone gives her the woolies, I understand she feels uncomfortable and needs to get away quickly. No further explanation is necessary.

Another expression we use in our home is "too wide open." This means being blindsided, causing us to become ungrounded. As an adult, you may experience being wide open when you're unexpectedly called into the boss's office, only to be criticized—or worse yet, let go. It can happen when you pick up the phone and someone "lets you have it." You know the feeling: overwhelmed, caught off guard, and surprised by someone's negative or intense energy.

My family also refers to "zipping up," which is a way of protecting yourself from unwanted influences, like zipping up your tent to keep out a hungry bear. I was with Sonia at the airport one day, waiting to check in luggage, when the man in front of us threw a fit at the counter. He was causing such a scene over his reservation mix-up that he'd gotten three ticket agents involved, and now they were beginning to argue among themselves. Their agitation was spilling over to the crowd of waiting passengers, who were starting to yell at him to "shut up" and "move on." It was an ugly situation and getting worse. Without a second thought, Sonia turned to me and said, "Uh-oh... trouble. Better zip up and ignore it." And she was right. Otherwise, we would have absorbed the tension like the people around us.

Using simple expressions such as the ones I discussed above sends the message to your subconscious mind that your intuition is important and needs to be heeded. It says, "I believe you," "I recognize this energy as real," and—most of all—"Act. Don't wait. Respond now to this information."

If you can't think of words to describe your intuitive feelings, make them up. People do it all the time. After all, it's your language. For example, thanks to the Marvel Comics character Spider-Man, many people now express their intuition as their "Spidey" sense, just as this character does. Enough people have adapted this term to describe intuition that it is now even finding its way into corporate America. For example, my client Lynn just shared that in her corporate job in health care, when her boss mentioned, "My Spidey sense is going off," they all sat up and paid attention.

Another term I've used is "ick attack." Its meaning is instantly clear—the icky or disgusted feeling you get around someone or something with highly unpleasant energy. For example, my daughter recently came back from visiting a potential preschool for her two-year-old daughter. When I asked her how she liked it, she said, "The building and classrooms were nice enough, but the school's principal gave me a major ick attack, so we are going to pass."

"Good idea," I responded, fully knowing what she meant and agreeing wholeheartedly.

More potent than an ick attack is a "psychic attack." This is when someone or something tries to intentionally hurt you with their energy. This occurs all the time. It's the ambush from the co-worker who wants your job, the flaky friend who blames you for his mistake, the malicious neighbor who competes with you, or the alcoholic in a rage. This term describes mean-spirited, harmful behavior that's directed toward you. It's real and imperative to guard yourself against. Naming it gives you the power to recognize a psychic attack for what it is, a hurtful assault, and invites you to protect yourself when it occurs. Naming a psychic attack also acts as a huge form of protection. Most psychic attackers are sneaky snipers who count on you, not recognizing their foul energy. Outing their sneaky assaults is often enough to stop them from harming you.

Your Words Are the Right Ones for You

Because of my background, it's natural for me to talk about intuition, ick attacks, and so forth but also about energy fields, auras, chakras, and other energy-based concepts. Although this vocabulary works well for me, it could be more valuable for you to create your own words to comfortably express your super sense in action. For example, you may prefer to refer to your intuition with more spiritual terms, such as "my angels" or "Spirit." Or you may like more everyday phrases, including "my gut," "my hunch," or "my feeling." One person I know calls a psychic attack a "stink bomb," while another describes an ick attack as a "yucky feeling." Yet another has chosen to name their intuition their "radar." The point is you can and should invent your own expressions to acknowledge your intuition. Maybe you already have. There are no "right" words to describe your intuition, only words that feel right for you.

Today's Jump Start

Today, select your own intuitive vocabulary to describe your super sense and what it is communicating to you. For example, you might say, "My vibes tell me to take some time to relax today" or "My gut tells me that it's best to not take that job offer." The key is not caring how the person you are speaking to reacts. The point is that for you, intuition is normal. The more you openly speak of your inner guidance without fear or hesitation, the stronger it shows up. Better yet, write down your favorite expressions for:

- an intuitive feeling

- a positive vibe

- a negative vibe

- feeling energetically uncomfortable

- a psychic attack

- a "Spidey" sense

- the woolies

- an ick attack

- any other intuitive experiences you wish to describe

Then use these words as you need to. After all, when you name it, you claim it.

DAY 10

Be Honest

I recently did a poll on my social media platforms asking over 300,000 people why they didn't listen to their intuition even when it spoke to them loud and clear. One of the top three responses I received was because people didn't want to hear what their intuition had to say if it didn't agree with what they wanted to hear. Lots of people, it seems, would rather pretend everything is the way they want to believe it is over acknowledging a disappointing truth. This is called denial. I wasn't surprised by this response. In my experience teaching intuition for as long as I have, I've observed firsthand how committed some people can be to denying the truth, even when contrary evidence smacks them in the face.

Several years ago, I met with a client named Pam who had come to see me because she had just inherited a significant amount of money and was about to go into business with her new boyfriend, a therapist whom Pam insisted was her soulmate. She then shared how they planned to start a healing retreat center, using her money to finance it.

Pam wanted my confirmation that they were soulmates and the retreat plan was their shared purpose in life. I wish I could have done that, but I saw quite another reality: her boyfriend was an opportunist, exploiting Pam's loneliness and her windfall. It wasn't love and destiny at all. It was an emotional and financial robbery. Seeing the lovestruck stars in her eyes, I gently suggested Pam separate the business and her money from their personal connection to ensure these were not crisscrossed before going forward with their plans. Then I asked her if she had any inkling that her relationship was not quite the ideal love match even though her boyfriend was strongly pushing for a long-term commitment. Despite the outer enthusiasm they shared, something was so energetically "off" that I wondered how she could not sense it.

"Has it occurred to you, Pam, that your boyfriend's motives and affection for you might be colored by the money you're offering him?" I ventured.

Deeply offended, she jerked up in her seat and snapped, "How dare you?" Then she stood up and stormed out.

I was saddened to see her reaction but not surprised. I knew her intuition told her the same thing. She just didn't want to hear it.

Eighteen months later, to my surprise, Pam booked another session with me. This time she showed up looking dejected and lost. She told me that after she'd spent over half a million dollars on her ex-boyfriend, he took off with another woman, not to be heard from again. Her dream of a healing center never materialized, her money disappeared, and she was totally humiliated. "Why didn't you warn me, Sonia? Didn't you see this coming?"

Flabbergasted, I said, "I tried to warn you, Pam. You just didn't want to hear it, remember?" She didn't.

More than not wanting to acknowledge other people's bad behavior, people ignore their intuition when it suggests that their own behavior is the problem. Unwilling to admit their errors in judgment, they bury their heads in the sands of denial while pretending all is well.

My client John, a friendly but easily manipulated guy, often ignored his inner guidance and went along with the crowd because, as he explained in our session, "It was easier." John was married to a low-key woman, Adrienne, and the father of a beautiful three-year-old daughter. John was invited to join his co-workers for drinks at the bar across the street at the end of each workday as a trader. John always accepted, wanting to be "one of the guys," even though his inner guidance said, "Bad idea." Ignoring this intuitive red light night after night, John regularly stayed too long, drank too much, and came home way too late to his wife and daughter. Not wanting to upset their daughter when John did show up, Adrienne didn't make a loud scene about his nightly tardiness, so John rationalized that it was okay. He ignored her low-toned disgust toward his absence and drinking and how she quickly ran out of patience with him.

One night at the bar, John had a powerful intuition to leave that very minute and go home, but instead of listening, he called Adrienne and offered another flimsy excuse. Getting her voice mail, John told himself, as usual, that everything was okay when, in his gut, he knew it wasn't. Denying his bad vibe, John stupidly (in his own words) stayed at the bar for another hour. When he finally did get home, John found the house dark and a note from Adrienne on the kitchen table saying she had taken their daughter and left him. John knew in his heart that if he had heeded his gut feeling when it overcame him an hour earlier and had come home right then, Adrienne would have still been there and maybe would have changed her mind. But sadly, denying his inner guidance on all those occasions cost him his marriage.

As you can see, our super sense often acts as a bright red light of protection, alerting us to dangerous behavior—our own and other people's—before it's too late. Ignoring this inner alarm is never a good idea.

However, our super sensor works as a bright green light of positivity and possibility, pushing us in the direction of what is good for us if we allow it to. I have a client, Kayla, who met Adam at an improv class in California 11 years ago. The minute they connected, she intuitively knew Adam was the guy to marry, even though he "looked terrible on paper," as she explained it. He had no money and inconsistent temporary work, and he wanted to be an actor but was unsuccessful. Kayla, on the other hand, was an only child from a prosperous real estate family. For her parents, money and social status were top priorities. Kayla knew they would reject Adam outright as a potential marriage partner, and she was right. They did.

Still, Kayla's super sense insisted he was "the one." She initially listened to her intuition over her parents' objections. But eventually, she stopped. She loved her parents (and the comfort their money brought her), so she ultimately decided to ignore her green light with Adam and "be practical," as her parents insisted she be. As a result, Kayla broke off her relationship with Adam. He was stunned, heartbroken, and angered, especially when she told him, "It's for the best," which both she and Adam knew was a lie.

Kayla went on to date others but never again found a love like the one she had with Adam. In time, Adam moved on and became a regularly featured actor in movies and television and enjoyed a successful life in the work he loved. He eventually married and had four boys. Years later, when Kayla came to see me for an intuitive reading, she said, "I only have one question, Sonia. Should I have married Adam, as my intuition told me to do back then?"

I responded, "Your intuition is your best guide, Kayla, but as you've learned, you are free to listen or ignore it. Unfortunately, you chose to ignore your inner guidance and listened to your family instead. Sadly, you regret it. However, it's best to forgive yourself and move on. There is more joy ahead if you are open to it. Learn your lesson and follow your heart going forward. That's all you can do." I knew Kayla would struggle with this. But I hoped she would succeed.

The bottom line is your inner guidance and heart tell the truth. If you want your super sense to work for you, you must be honest with yourself and listen to the truth even when it's inconvenient, uncomfortable, or disappointing. You always have a choice. You don't have to follow your inner guidance, but at least hear it out. The cost of ignoring it may be too high.

Today's Jump Start

Be honest with yourself today.

In what way, if any, are you resistant to hearing what your super sense has to say? Is there any area where you avoid the truth of a situation or relationship? Even with yourself?

Answer out loud.

While acknowledging everything your intuition reveals may not be easy, denial is worse. It is far better to face any temporary disappointment or challenge that comes with being honest over the long-term damage that comes from walking into trouble or away from an opportunity because you weren't willing to see the signals in advance.

DAY 11

Write It Down

It goes without saying that your intuition is useless if you don't trust it. Most people I've met want to trust their super sense but don't because they're afraid to. Fear of all sorts is the number one reason why people don't trust their intuition. Over and over, I hear, "What if I make a mistake?" "What if my intuition is wrong?" or "What if something awful happens because my intuition is off?" "What if my intuition leads me off a cliff?" "What if I hurt someone by trusting my intuition? Or make them angry?" The list of fears goes on, so intuition goes unheeded. These fears present possible scenarios, but if you listen to your intuition and not your fears, they start to subside, replaced by the confidence and courage to be yourself.

Trusting your intuition is a risk you'll eventually take if you want to activate your super sense and begin using your full power. If you ask me, ignoring your inner guidance and allowing your fearful ego to run your life is far riskier. I can't think of a single example of a person's unwarranted fear leading to a positive outcome. But I can think of endless examples of one's fearful ego bringing on the worst possible results.

Still, I get it. Standing behind your intuitive feelings without evidence to support them is a significant responsibility and can be challenging. But listening to your intuition doesn't have to be a blind leap into the chaotic unknown that your ego tries to convince you it is. Instead, you can learn to trust your intuition the same way you do anything else in life: gradually, through positive, consistent experience.

The best way to overcome the fear of trusting your inner guidance is to get a small pocket notebook you can carry around. Whenever you get a hunch, gut feeling, an "Aha!" feeling, a hit, a sense, a vibe, or any other nudge from your super sense, jot it down in your notebook. Don't let your ego censor, judge, discriminate, interfere with, or in any way edit the intuitive information or feelings you receive. And don't worry if your inner guidance feels silly, irrelevant, irrational, or stupid or it makes no sense or if you think your intuition is nothing more than your imagination. Write it all down anyway. Then wait.

At this point, you don't have to follow your intuition. Simply record instead of ignoring your super sense and see if it proves to be worth trusting in time. In a short while, with that notebook to refer to, you will soon discover that every vibe you have will eventually make sense in one way or another. If you record your intuition faithfully for even a week, your fears and doubts will give way to confidence in your super sense because you will have collected solid, undeniable evidence that your super sense is worth trusting.

Getting Started

For some, recognizing your intuition, let alone recording it, may seem daunting because up until now, you've habitually "stuffed" it. But guess what: writing down your guidance quickly eases such confusion and intimidation. For example, my client Maya said:

I used to automatically strangle my intuition before I knew what it was trying to tell me. If I felt the slightest bit uneasy, rather than recognizing my hunch as a warning, I'd immediately go in the opposite direction, convincing myself that I was crazy. I'd intentionally distract myself from chasing away these troubled feelings by scrolling on social media or shopping online. Inevitably, my uneasiness would eventually prove to be an accurate warning of things to come, but because I ignored it, it did me no good. This hindsight drove me crazy. Once I stopped stuffing my super sense and began writing down my intuitive flashes, they got increasingly sharper and more specific. With this, my anxiety decreased because I saw these feelings protected me. The more I wrote, the more what started as a vague notion, like "Bad feeling about my employee Laura," turned into a full-blown clear understanding of what was wrong. "Laura is lying to me about the amount of time she puts into work from home and is charging me for not even being there." Within days of beginning to record my intuitive feelings in my notebook, I tuned in to specific scenarios with incredible accuracy, which made life better in the long run. It was mind-boggling.

My client Christine told me that writing down her intuitive feelings helped her music career take off:

The more I wrote, the more complete song lyrics intuitively dropped in. Soon I was downloading entire melodies and even guidance on how to find people who could help me record, arrange, and produce my songs. Finally, six months after recording my intuitive feelings in a notebook, I produced my first CD after years of wasting time producing nothing. I'm still amazed this has happened.

Anna, a chronically fearful, self-doubting client, started writing down her intuitive feelings twice daily, once at lunchtime and the second before bed. At first, she said she felt ridiculous, as if she were making things up and rambling on about nonsense. Anna felt so silly, she even hid her notebook and intentionally didn't write her name in it in case someone else discovered it. "Still, writing in this notebook for only five minutes daily changed me," she said.

I stopped criticizing myself like I used to do. And once I started writing about what bothered me and asked my intuition to guide me, I began to feel calmer and more confident. Better yet, I quickly discovered that just underneath my fear, I got clear guidance that proved helpful and exciting. For example, three months ago, I wrote in my notebook that a new neighbor I casually met for only a minute would be important in my life. After that, it was just a vibe. Two months later, we spent the entire day together working in our community garden, and by the end of the day, we had bonded. Now we are dating, and I've never been happier. I knew the minute we met there was a connection, but writing it down solidified it. I recently showed him this entry in my journal, and he laughed and said he'd had the same feeling when he met me.

Writing down what your super sense communicates is the most effective way to shift from fear to confidence when trusting your intuition. Your certainty will increase with each recorded message from your intuition. You'll no longer just have a vague feeling—you'll have solid verification that your super sense is a legitimate guide you can count on.

Keeping a journal also tells your subconscious mind that you value your intuition. Every time you write something down, you validate it, even (and especially) if what you write down doesn't make immediate sense to your logical brain. It trains your mind not to dismiss or ignore these subtle messengers because they will make sense eventually. It doesn't take long for your subconscious to cooperate and increase the volume of your intuition.

If you've been trained to ignore your super sense, recording your intuitive feelings on paper, your computer, or your smartphone will "untrain" you and restore this empowering connection to your true Self. Fortunately, your higher channel never stops broadcasting guidance on your path. It is your attention that stops noticing or tunes out the messages. Intuition is a natural and integral part of who you are as a spiritual being. Being so disconnected from your super sense is so unnatural that you don't trust or even feel it. Writing down your intuition repairs this disconnection from your Spirit and reassures you of your personal competence and power to successfully lead your life.

Today's Jump Start

Buy a small notebook or use a notes application on your smartphone to record your intuitive feelings. Choose whichever one is easiest to carry with you everywhere. Pull it out once or twice today and record what your intuition is telling you. If you do not sense anything to write, ask your intuition for guidance and write that down. Record every hunch, "Aha!" hit, vibe, or intuitive sense you've had all day. A few words are enough. "Good intuition at the meeting," "Bad feeling from my sister's new boyfriend," and so on is all you need. Just write enough to capture what you feel and validate your super sense. You don't have to write an essay, although one might spontaneously come through.

Your Spirit has much to share and will if it can. So don't stop after today. Keep going. If you do, in time, this little notebook will be the best book you've ever read because it will contain the story of how you reclaimed your super sense and personal power once and for all.

DAY 12

Dare to Be Different

To successfully jump-start your intuition, you must be willing to be different from others at times and accept intuition as normal for you, even if it isn't for them. That might feel like a big challenge, especially if others have treated you poorly regarding your super sense. However, if you've had bad experiences around your super sense (and most of us have), it is time to let go of the past, move on, and regain your power.

Accepting intuition as your "normal" makes sense, and you may think you already do. Yet, are you sure? I've been teaching people to turn on their intuition for almost 50 years, and in that time, I've observed that tuning in to intuition is not the biggest challenge for most people—at least not for those in my classes (and probably not for you either, because you are reading this book). Your intuition is likely already turned on, at least to some degree. The biggest challenge lies in feeling totally secure and comfortable with having and using six fully operational senses, especially if you've been told that having a super sense is super weird.

I get it. People sometimes treat you as though having a sixth, super sense is like having six fingers or an extra ear. Because it isn't yet considered "normal" for many people, you may want to hide it away. If someone around you considers your intuition "weird," "strange," "funny," "scary," "bizarre," "woo-woo," or worse, you do risk being rejected. To avoid this discomfort, you may find yourself denying your intuition exists or hiding it.

I recently met a woman named Lucy at a fundraiser, and we began to chat. After I told her I helped people develop their intuition, she immediately said, almost repulsed, "That's not for me." Then she launched into how she used to be very intuitive when she was young, especially sensing people's hidden motives for what they were. But her father would have none of that. Instead, he yelled, "That's not normal, Lucy. Stop talking like that," whenever she spoke up about her intuition. So she stopped sharing it because of his reaction. Some version of Lucy's story is familiar. It's probably the most common one I've heard over the years. We all have six senses, even if some deny this, but a negative experience like the one Lucy suffered takes a toll, causing an almost involuntary distancing from our super sense if we let it.

I have a gay client named Liz who has taken classes from me over the years and is now an intuitive coach for others herself. "Because I'm gay, I know what being different is like. Some people simply cannot accept this difference and judge me. But not everyone. Almost everyone judges me for being psychic, though!" I laughed hard at this because it is so true. When it comes to owning up to a strong sixth sense, rejection from others cuts across the board.

But it doesn't have to. Consider someone else's limited view an invitation for you to overcome a need for approval. There is no need to feel hurt, defensive, scared, combative, or secretive around people who don't get you. It's about them and not you.

So, how do you avoid these feelings? With self-love and humor. That's right. Love and accept yourself unconditionally and have a sense of humor even when others don't. Rather than fear other people's judgments, recognize them for what they are—lack of understanding of your spiritual nature and intuitive capacity—and know that their judgments are not about you.

Moreover, don't bang your head against a wall trying to change anyone's perception or comfort level with intuition, because it is an inside job. You can't influence another person's opinion on the topic; only having a positive personal experience of one's own intuition can do that. This will happen to everyone eventually. We are all evolving into six-sense beings. In the meantime, smile in the face of adversaries and say, with confidence, "Well, it seems we're different." And nothing more. The more you are at ease with your intuition, the more others will be. If you need another person's approval, you won't get it. If you don't, it comes. In any case, consider that what matters most is your own self-approval and being true to yourself.

My client Bernadette is a highly psychic veterinarian. She listens to her intuition when she works with animals and communicates telepathically with her animal patients in her practice all the time, and it's no secret. Some of her clients love and appreciate this. Others don't. "Yesterday," she shared, "a woman and her two grown daughters brought in an 18-year-old poodle because he was barely moving. Tests revealed he had several small tumors on his throat and tongue. My intuition told me he was in excruciating pain and was suffering terribly. He asked me to help him die so he could be released. The daughters begged me to do everything to keep him alive, but the suffering poodle said, 'Please don't.'"

Bernadette shared with the three women what the poodle wanted, and the two daughters had a fit. One rolled her eyes, and the other screamed, "That's not real." But the mother and owner of the dog said, "Thank you. I feel the same way. He is ready to go. Please help him." In the end, the poodle was put to sleep, and Bernadette felt peaceful because she had served the Spirit of this dog in the best possible way. Yet the drama she had to endure as she followed her super sense was, in her words, "no fun."

At times, being intuitive can be no fun. But you can try to make it as fun as possible whenever appropriate. (Putting a beloved pet to sleep is never fun.) When someone calls you a weirdo, you can agree by saying, "So true. Thank you for noticing" or "That's what I love the most about myself." In other words, catch people off guard. If you don't react to people's judgments, they relax and become curious. Eventually, they may even come around to accepting it.

My client Stefano openly shares with everyone he knows what his Spidey sense says. He even refers to his intuition as "Spidey," and now so do his friends. "Last week, when out with friends, I was asked three times to consult Spidey for advice. Everyone acts like it's a joke, but I know they are serious. They see how well my Spidey sense works and want it to work for them too."

Today's Jump Start

Take a day off from seeking other people's approval, especially when you have a fully functioning sixth sense that you count on and openly acknowledge. Start by not automatically asking others what they think, unless it is necessary, such as when you at work and asking your boss. The minute you ask others what they think, you give your power away and often to people who don't have any idea what you need or what is important to you, let alone care.

Moreover, we often get very direct and accurate intuitive guidance but tend to handle it like a hot potato, throwing it into someone else's lap for approval before we even consider what it has to offer for ourselves. Today resolve not to do this, and reverse yourself quickly if you do. For example, if you do automatically ask for someone's approval, say, "I'm sorry. I didn't mean to put this on you. I know what to do," even if you aren't sure. Simply reversing this tendency gives you the courage and strength to follow your heart, and surprisingly you will know what to do.

Secondly, at the beginning of the day, resolve that if you do receive disapproval on something that intuitively speaks to you, you are prepared to deflect the energy. Say something like "Thanks for your feedback, but I'm trusting my vibes on this anyway and am willing to stand by it." Then change the subject. This is a clear way of letting people know their approval isn't necessary and their disapproval won't deter you.

Expect negative feedback or disapproval but don't allow them to keep you from following your inner guidance. Of course, this requires you take 100 percent responsibility for what you choose to follow, but that's always better than following the random opinions of others. Listen to your heart, choose to follow it, and pray for courage if you are afraid or hesitant. My favorite daily prayer of intention is "Spirit, move me toward my highest good this day." If you say this aloud and mean it, you will be moved, no matter what disapproval you may encounter from others or any hesitation you may have. By following your guidance despite disapproval, you let others know you love and accept yourself unconditionally and honor your super sense completely. It states that while you don't have all the answers, you are willing to give your heart a chance to find them.

As an aside, there are those whom you may want to seek guidance from. These include wise elders, teachers, guides, and therapists. However, a good guide in any capacity will always encourage you to listen to and follow your heart and be true to yourself. If the guidance you receive diminishes your power, responsibility, or authenticity, then it isn't good guidance; it is manipulation.

DAY 13

Read the Room

A significant and practical part of being intuitive involves being aware of the energy around you and how it affects you and others. After all, as quantum physics now affirms, we are energetic beings constantly interacting with one another on an energetic level, both locally and at a distance. When we interact with positive energy, we feel great. When we interact with negative energy, we become agitated and drained.

For example, have you ever entered a room shortly after an argument? If you are the least bit sensitive, chances are you feel tension and anger lingering in the air, causing you to naturally contract your muscles and even hold your breath a little, shoring up your defenses. On the other hand, have you ever walked into a beautiful church, temple, or mosque and immediately felt a wave of peace and relaxation sweep over you? Or walked into a fine restaurant and, despite its good reviews, immediately sensed that you wouldn't enjoy your experience because the atmosphere was too uptight, all without anyone saying a word?

Of course, we've all had these experiences, but some of us rarely give them the attention they deserve. Some of us carry on, denying what we feel as if everything were okay when it's not. At best, this leaves us feeling phony, and at worst, it can put us in danger.

Many of us have been taught to deny what we feel, so naturally, this creates internal chaos and stress. This is especially true of children, whose hearts and energy fields are more open than those of more defensive adults and who are often and sadly told by adults that what they feel isn't real. For example, how would you feel if you saw a bus coming straight toward you and you were about to get hit, while a well-intending adult told you the bus wasn't there? What would you do? Denying someone's intuition or telling someone who is accurately reading a place, person, or situation that what they sense isn't real teaches them to doubt themselves at the deepest level. It's so damaging. It's equally damaging when you do this to yourself.

For example, I spoke with a client, Marilyn, who shared that she and her husband were snarled in daily battles and had been for some time. Their fights were so bad, they recently decided to divorce. She called me for a session because, on top of dealing with this crisis, their ten-year-old son, Hudson, recently developed ongoing severe stomach pains. "I'm so afraid something is horribly wrong with him," she said, genuinely confused. "But the doctors can't find a thing so far. He is scheduled for more serious tests tomorrow, and I'm scared. I fear the worst."

What was wrong was immediately evident to me, and I was struck by Marilyn's lack of perception. "Is Hudson aware of your impending divorce?" I asked. Shocked, she answered, "Not at all! We haven't said a word to him. He doesn't know a thing, and we don't want him to, either, especially since he feels so sick."

"You are wrong about him not knowing anything," I answered. "He may not have been told the truth by you two, but he intuitively feels it anyway, and it's causing him tremendous anxiety. Pretending everything is okay when clearly it isn't only makes him confused, so he is stuffing his intuition, and it pains him. He is sickened by both the toxic energy in the house and the fact that you two deny it, leaving him questioning what or whom to trust. Surely you must have considered this."

She looked shocked. "No way! Do you think so? We've been so careful around him."

"You have been carefully pretending, but Hudson senses this is a lie. I certainly believe this is playing a big part in whatever is happening to his stomach," I replied. Ignoring or denying what we perceive doesn't make the energy go away. Good or bad, if not acknowledged consciously, the energy we are experiencing gets trapped in our organs.

Later, Marilyn shared that Hudson's diagnosis was "general stress." With that information following our conversation, Marilyn, her husband, and Hudson began family therapy. I'm unsure what happened to Hudson after that, but at least he was no longer being gaslit by denial and pretense.

Are You Reading the Room or Denying It?

Marilyn's son isn't the only one who is reading the room. We all are. It is part of our hardwiring as intuitive beings. We need to as a survival mechanism. It protects us to use our super sense to confirm what our outer senses cannot register or what is intentionally being hidden from us.

Maya Angelou, the great American poet, once said, "When someone shows you who they are, believe them the first time." This means not only what they outwardly show you but what they energetically reveal as well.

The key to knowing if you are using your intuition instead of simply projecting onto others is to pay attention to what you actually notice. Real intuition is short, direct, and to the point, leaving you feeling relieved, informed, strengthened, and clear. In contrast, a negative ego judgment or projection is often long-winded, rambling, competitive, righteous, and usually leaves you feeling yucky.

When intuitively assessing people and places, avoid interpreting things too simplistically as merely "good" or "bad." People or situations that make you feel "good" do so because they relay positive or harmonious vibrations to you, whereas people or situations that make you feel "bad" may be draining your energy because their energy is just not harmonious with yours. It isn't that one type is good and another bad or that what you feel reflects how a person or situation always is. It may reflect the moment alone.

Study energy neutrally, then respond accordingly. For example, if you are around a draining force, you can move away, cut the conversation short, or redirect that person's attention. By being aware, you give yourself choices and maintain your power. If you are unaware or are not paying attention to how people or situations affect you, you put yourself at a disadvantage. For example, you may not notice you are being drained by someone until you feel like you want to pass out. Or you may unintentionally drain the next person down the line as you try to regain the energy you've just lost. In that case, this unsuspecting next person will consider you the negative, draining one. So, you see, the more you intuitively assess the energy of people, places, and situations you find yourself connecting to, the more informed, empowered, and protected you will be.

Today's Jump Start

Stop and read the vibe of the room right now. Set aside this book and close your eyes. Take a deep breath and listen to the vibration of the place. What does it tell you? This isn't a test, so don't worry about not getting it "right." Imagine you're doing something as simple and routine as checking the weather, and trust your immediate assessment.

Intuitively read any people who might be in the room or were recently in the room and their energy is still there. Say what you feel quickly and out loud (or as loud as you can without causing offense). Don't overthink, and don't judge. Trust your first impressions, as they are usually the most accurate. Listen with your whole body and not your ears alone. What do you sense, and how does it leave you feeling? Express it out loud. After you express what you intuitively feel, notice how it affects you on the inside. Does what you intuitively read ring true in your body? Does it feel accurate? Does what you sense leave you feeling relaxed and satisfied? Is it unquestionably clear, or does it leave you confused and second-guessing?

The quicker and clearer your "intuitive read," the more accurate it is and the more empowered you will feel. You will get better at this with practice. If you find yourself second-guessing or overthinking as you try this, that's a sign that your ego has taken over this exercise. Stop for now and try again later.

DAY 14

Speak Up

By now, you know we have six senses, not five, and are naturally intuitive. We regularly receive subtle (and sometimes not so subtle) intuitive messages all the time. Even so, when our super sense sounds an alarm, some people still refuse to speak up because they are unwilling to face the potential adverse opinions and reactions of others that often follow. They worry they might hurt someone's feelings, disappoint others, be accused of being uncooperative or a troublemaker, be made to feel like they are ruining the party or upsetting the status quo, or worse. They fear that breaking from the group and standing apart will make them look like a fool or uncool with no possible recovery. So they keep quiet.

This all boils down to one basic problem: being a people pleaser over being true to yourself. Being a people pleaser and silencing your inner guidance comes with a price. It chips away at your self-esteem, diminishes your integrity, and leaves you feeling inauthentic. Yes, it can be hard to share your vibes when you know you will be met with resistance, but is it worth losing your integrity and self-esteem not to?

Evelyn had to decide. After college, Evelyn went into business with her lifelong best friend, Sarah, creating a software consulting company at Sarah's urging. Evelyn loved Sarah's confidence, even though, at times, she found Sarah too impulsive, which overwhelmed her. However, Sarah's can-do spirit worked in their favor most of the time and helped their company get off the ground. Evelyn was glad to follow Sarah's headlong approach to life and let her lead because it usually worked well. That is, until Sarah started dating Tom, a guy she met on a dating app.

Even though Tom did nothing outwardly questionable to suggest he couldn't be trusted, Evelyn's danger signals went off whenever Tom came around. Fortunately for Evelyn, it wasn't often, so she kept quiet and didn't share her suspicions even though she wanted to. It made Evelyn uncomfortable to watch Sarah get in deeper and deeper with Tom, but it made her more uncomfortable to speak up and share her negative feelings and possibly make Sarah angry. So she said nothing.

Within a few months, Sarah moved in with Tom, further setting Evelyn on edge. Something about Tom was way "off," and Evelyn knew it, but she had nothing more than her intuition to back her up. Evelyn didn't mention her concerns to Sarah but did mention them to her husband, Jack. Only, he laughed, told her she was being overly protective, and insisted Tom was great, so that didn't help. Evelyn pushed her vibes further aside, although it was almost painful to do this.

When the wedding date was set, Sarah asked Evelyn to be her maid of honor, and Evelyn knew it was time to speak up about her bad vibes. But Sarah seemed so happy, and Evelyn did not want to ruin her best friend's joy. Evelyn knew she was being a chicken by keeping quiet but rationalized that Sarah was an adult and knew what she was doing and didn't ask for input, so Evelyn didn't offer it.

The wedding came, and all seemed well, but shortly after, Sarah came into work with bruises on her face and arms. Horrified, Evelyn asked what had happened, and Sarah explained she had fallen at home. Evelyn knew it was a lie but again said nothing. Another month passed, and Sarah showed up with a broken wrist, again saying she'd fallen, but this time Evelyn snapped. She couldn't keep quiet a minute longer. "Sarah, I don't believe you. What did Tom do?"

Sarah then broke down crying and confessed that Tom would occasionally get drunk, and when he did, he lost his temper and sometimes ended up being violent. Sarah insisted he was a wonderful man otherwise but had been under pressure lately because he'd recently lost his job, which provoked his violent behavior.

Evelyn felt sick. If she had spoken up, she wondered, maybe Sarah would have been more honest with herself about Tom's addictions and violent tendencies before they married. Instead, Evelyn shook her head. "I knew Tom was not a good guy, Sarah. I just didn't know how to tell you—you seemed so happy. I don't care how much pressure he is under. He's dangerous. Get out now."

Sarah became angry with Evelyn, refused to leave Tom, and things spiraled downward fast. Sarah became more battered, and Evelyn became more frustrated, helplessly watching from the sidelines. In less than a year, Sarah left the business and moved out of town with Tom to another state, where he got a new job. Evelyn was heartsick because she had failed her friend by being quiet. "I not only failed Sarah, but I also failed myself," Evelyn confessed when she came for a reading. "I didn't want to make Sarah angry or myself uncomfortable, so I kept quiet and fed her to a wolf."

Evelyn was not responsible for Sarah's decisions, but she was responsible for her own. Silencing her intuition to keep the peace is a form of self-betrayal that keeps us from living in our full power and integrity, and that's what bothered Evelyn the most.

It is understandable why so many people feel this way. Speaking up and sharing your inner guidance can be unpopular with other people, especially if your vibes involve them. This is because your inner guidance can be disruptive for someone. Even Evelyn's husband shut her down with his response. So the question is, who will you disrupt? Others or your own integrity?

When our intuition senses something that could be unpopular with someone else (and it will), we must be willing to face their disapproval. I call facing this "dancing in the fire" because disapproval can feel that intense. And yet, if we energetically dance instead of people please, if we stay true to ourselves and keep listening to our heart and Spirit instead of saying what will appeal to other people, we will eventually become immune to other people's disapproval and elevate our own self-esteem and approval, which is so much better.

It's necessary to be prepared to dance in the fire of negative opinion if you want to be an intuitively empowered, authentic person. This is inevitable because people will push back. For them, it's easier to try to shut you down than to change their direction. Don't let this intimidate you. Speak up anyway.

Today's Jump Start

Today, bravely stay true to yourself and speak up if you have vibes that need to be shared, even if it means potentially facing disapproval or other adverse reactions. A go-to phrase for most challenges is "I trust my intuition. It works for me." Often that is enough said, but if you must say more, simply add "My intuition has proven to be a reliable guide for me [always emphasize the 'me' part], so I'm choosing to follow it even if it doesn't make logical sense right now."

Expect pushback and be prepared for others to get annoyed, even angry, especially if your vibes interfere with how they want things to unfold. For example, if you are being pushed to go somewhere, do something, or agree with something that doesn't feel right for you, like staying out when your vibes say, "Go home," or spending money when your vibes say, "Not on this," or hearing "He's such a great guy" when your vibes say, "He's a con," respect your intuition by simply saying things like "I'm sorry it's disappointing, but I have to follow my vibes" or "That doesn't work for me. I have a different vibe on this." Then smile.

Expect to be accused of being negative, a party pooper, or the one "raining on the parade" at times because intuition often suggests a change of plans, and people don't like that. Also expect to be laughed at or encouraged to ignore and betray your feelings to "keep the peace" because intuition is honest, and some people aren't interested in being that honest.

There is no way around it: One important and protective facet of intuition is that it is a disrupter. It is a good one but nevertheless often an unwanted one. It goes with the territory to disrupt poor plans when living an empowered, intuitive life.

The point is don't let anything stop you from being true to yourself. Don't argue with anyone, either. It's useless and futile. If you're accused of being crazy or no fun, agree! Say, "Yes, I know I'm a bit crazy, but I always go with my vibes" with a smile instead of getting defensive or angry in kind. This usually stops the pushback, if not the grumbling. I've found you must stand up for yourself and your decision to follow your inner guidance only one or two times before others get the message that this is what they can expect of you, and so they stop trying to get you to abandon yourself.

Generally, only those who are disconnected from their intuition, who don't know or want to know how to be honest with themselves, tell you to abandon your vibes because it's easier for them than acknowledging what they are denying. However, the price for pleasing such people over stating your true feelings is high. The cost is your personal power and self-respect.

So, even if it causes upset, listen to your inner guidance and speak up when necessary. Don't overexplain your intuition to anyone. Be clear and direct: "I trust my intuition no matter what." And mean it. People can tell by your vibration if you do. When you make that choice and stand by it, you reclaim your integrity, autonomy, and personal power and are liberated from the control of the outside world. You may lose a friend or two (or even family) or experience some tension or distance, but it's better than having relationships that insist you ignore your super sense just to keep them comfortable. In the end you gain the respect of others, if not their approval. It can be a challenge, but one worth facing. Once you commit to listening to your intuition, you become the true leader of your life. Wasn't that the goal of awakening your intuition all along?

Week 3

GROW IT

This week the adventure continues as you discover new ways to brainstorm for intuitive solutions, meet your strong, Divine support system, strengthen your intuitive muscles with powerful workouts, and experience more ease and joy knowing your intuition can be reliably counted on to guide you to success in every challenge you encounter, watching your fears fade and your confidence rise. By the end of the week, your sixth sense superpower will be fully operating, and you will be more empowered than ever.

DAY 15

Meet Your
Guardian Angel

As Divine beings, we have a Divine support system consisting of angels, guides, light beings, nature Spirits, and our Mother-Father God, ever present to assist and guide us through our lives, from our first breath to our last. This support system changes as we do. Our guardian angel, however, is always with us, while our Spirit guides come and go depending on our focus and growth. Many famous people throughout history spoke of their connection with a Spirit helper or guide. Perhaps one of the most famous is Carl Jung, a Swiss psychiatrist and founder of analytical psychology, a school of thought that has significantly influenced modern psychology and psychotherapy.

Jung spoke daily with a guide named Philemon. His guide first appeared during a series of active imagination experiences and visualizations Jung underwent in the early 20th century. Philemon appeared as an old man with a white beard, wearing a winged heart and carrying the keys to wisdom. He offered Jung guidance, insight, and a higher perspective than his ego and became a constant friend, companion, and source of intuitive inspiration throughout his life.

Jung spoke with Philemon in several ways, often during meditative visualization sessions where they conversed at length. Sometimes Jung conversed with Philemon by writing, asking questions and receiving answers. Communicating with Philemon was a big part of Jung's work throughout his life.

Socrates, an ancient Greek philosopher, also spoke of his Spirit guide Daimonion (not to be confused with our word "demon"), who guided him through his life, warning him against making mistakes, advising him on what path to take but never telling him directly what to do. In fact, the daimon was a big part of Greek culture, with each person having a Divine guiding presence throughout their life.

Growing up Catholic, I was raised with the understanding that we all had a wealth of guiding forces available to help us, starting with my guardian angel. I was introduced to legions of angels, saints, departed loved ones, light beings, nature spirits, elementals, and the Mother-Father God as easily as I was introduced to the neighbors. I've never had a day when I felt I was on my own. My Divine support system was perpetually on call for me. At home and at church, we prayed to our Divine helpers for intercession and support on every concern in the world, confident our prayers would be heard and answered. They were.

My personal Spirit guides and helpers initially appeared to me at the age of five or six. The first guide was Rose, a loving presence who appeared in my bedroom every night just as I fell asleep. She was and remains unconditionally loving and reassuring, letting me know I am never alone and I am always loved and deeply protected. I have many other Spirit guides and helpers, including Joseph, who helps with practical matters, like finding me homes and apartments, getting my car fixed (when I owned one), and keeping my family and me safe and secure when we travel. Then there is Joachim, a master teacher guide who helps me teach when I speak to groups. These are only a few members of my expansive Divine support system, which we all have and from which we all can receive guidance.

My friend Nancy was fascinated when I first introduced angels and guides to her. Raised in a nonreligious, nonspiritual household, the thought of having an unseen angelic support system gave her tremendous joy and reassurance. Nancy was especially drawn to the archangels, principal angels who oversee our lives and offer us powerful support and protection. I told her I playfully called the archangels "the archies" and surrounded myself with them in all six directions, above, below, front, back, and on both sides, whenever I left the house to ensure safe and joyful experiences throughout each day.

Nancy immediately took to "the archies" and adopted them as her own. They gave her an immediate sense of confidence she had never felt before. She also loved learning about guardian angels and called upon hers to step forward. "In my imagination, he appeared as a powerful and beautiful presence on a horse with a huge wingspan. He had a delightful laugh and introduced himself as Lancelot," she shared. "The minute Lancelot showed up, I felt as if I'd known him forever. With his support, I found the courage to start my consulting business, something I had wanted to do for years but was afraid to. With Lancelot and my Spirit guides on deck, I get answers, ideas, solutions, and inspirations that my ego was never creative or confident enough to offer me."

Accessing your guides is easy: Simply accept they are there and open your imagination to let them in. Don't let your ego get in the way by needing to know how this works. Just as there are entire schools of beautiful fish in the sea that you cannot see but know are there, so, too, is there an enchanting world of angels, guides, and Spirit helpers swimming in the subtle planes, surrounding you with love and support. Ask your ego to step aside and let your imagination take you there.

My client Stewart, a highly logical accountant, was skeptical when I told him he had a guardian angel waiting in the wings to help him. He smirked when I mentioned this and said it was an entertaining fantasy but, honestly, hard to believe. I smiled and asked him if he wanted a guardian angel.

He responded, "Sure. Who doesn't?"

So I answered, "Ask them to show up, choose a name so you can communicate, and request a sign that they are nearby, as you are a skeptic. I'm not going to try to convince you of their presence. If you want to meet them, you'll make it happen."

"Okay," he conceded, "so what do I do?"

"Close your eyes and tell me, on which side are they standing behind you?" I asked.

"On my left," he replied, playful and clearly making it up.

"What's their name?" I then inquired.

"Casper, like the friendly ghost." He smiled, then burst out laughing.

"Ask him for a sign to let you know he's here."

Despite feeling silly, Stewart cooperated, lifted his head, and said out loud, "Casper, if you're here, send me a sign." He left with that, shaking his head and saying it was fun but ridiculous.

The following day Stewart called, nearly breathless with surprise. "Guess what I found in my mailbox this morning! Ten white feathers with no note. This is crazy!"

"Not to me," I answered. "Casper didn't waste any time, did he?"

Today's Jump Start

Today, meet your guardian angel. Close your eyes and ask yourself, on which side is this gorgeous Divine helper standing by you? To the left or to the right? Sense your guardian angel's presence and point. Trust what you instantly feel, and don't question it. Once you connect, ask your guardian angel for their name and quickly say it aloud.

Take the first name that pops into your mind. Then say, "Hello. I'm glad you're here." Once this connection is made, let the relationship unfold.

If your imagination has a hiccup and you cannot feel your angel, choose the side you want your guardian angel to be on and instruct your angel to always meet you there. Your angel loves you and will do whatever you ask to feel connected. Again, if your imagination is a little rusty and you don't get a name after asking, make up your own name for your guardian angel and say, "This is what I'll call you when we communicate." That works too. The name is just a way to connect, and your angel is delighted to do this in any way that works for you.

Once you've made contact and have decided on a name, feel free to ask your angel to give you a sign they are near each day, and then be open to receiving one. The most common angel sign is a feather. Often one will show up soon after you consciously connect with your guardian angel.

DAY 16

Observe,
Don't Absorb

It's not enough that your intuition works; you want to be discerning with your intuitive radar. This is because unless you're discerning, you may unwittingly tune in and absorb energy you don't want and that isn't useful to you. As quantum physics asserts, we are made of energetic vibrations. This energy is like a radio frequency, and we all broadcast on different energy levels simultaneously. Think of the signals we broadcast when grounded in our Spirit as those of a classical-music satellite station—a beautiful relay of spiritual guidance and healing.

In contrast, when we are not in good energy, we broadcast much lower, more discordant energy or what I call "psychic riffraff." This unpleasant energetic broadcast transmits the negative vibration of our feelings, moods, fears, thoughts, anxieties, and even nightmares. Consider this psychic relay the equivalent of low-vibration A.M. talk radio. In other words, distressing noise.

If your intuitive channel is turned on but your tuner isn't dialed to what is important, valuable to, and harmonious with you, you may accidentally dial in to someone's low-vibration negative broadcast without knowing it and let it take over your body and mind.

For example, have you ever felt suddenly depressed or anxious when visiting an unhappy friend or family member, even though you were in a great mood when you arrived? Or walked into a room and suddenly felt agitated and impatient to leave? This may be because you've absorbed that person or place's anxiety, depression, or fear, causing your sudden change of mood and outlook. If unaware, you may absorb someone else's stress, anger, or even illness and suddenly feel irritated, exhausted, or drained for no reason. This can happen when you're with one person or in a group or a crowd, such as on public transportation or in a toxic office space.

As one client said in despair, "Sonia, I think I'm sponging up everyone's bad mood on the subway! By the time I get to work, I feel like I'm carrying the world's aches, pains, and worries in my body." She was. Another said, "The minute I walk into work, I instantly fall into a bad mood. It's like the office is poisoned with negative energy, and I am sickened by it."

Has this ever happened to you? Are you susceptible to absorbing other people's energy or getting doused by negative vibes when you're with certain people or in certain places? Think about it. How long before you take on the same energy when around an anxious, agitated person? For many, probably not long.

Children and teenagers are especially vulnerable to absorbing a toxic atmosphere, such as at school, where the tension and energy can be extremely low, and some try to say so. Only, they risk getting punished or ridiculed for being so frank, especially if the source of their bad vibes is unwilling to own their polluting energy.

When my daughter Sabrina was in preschool, for example, the teacher, Ms. Agnes, lost patience with the children and put the entire class of three-year-olds in time-out. Sitting quietly for a minute, Sabrina then stood up, straightened her dress, approached her teacher's desk, and said, "Ms. Agnes, we are feeling happy in the corner. When you feel better, would you like to join us?" Ms. Agnes was so taken aback that she didn't know whether to get angry with Sabrina or laugh.

Fortunately, she laughed as Sabrina was right: she was the one misbehaving. Being called out, Ms. Agnes released the kids and put herself in time-out, which was what was really called for that morning.

Luckily Sabrina was three, and Ms. Agnes found it cute as she recounted the episode to me when I picked Sabrina up that day. I'm quite sure had Sabrina been in middle or high school, the teacher's response would have likely been less positive, even punishing. Both adults and kids misbehave all the time because of fear, yet few of us are willing to admit it. That's too scary. It seems most prefer to attack, defend, blame, or retreat over acknowledging the true state of energy and where it's coming from.

I believe absorbing other people's negative energy plays a significant role in why sensitive children, teenagers, and adults feel so easily depressed all the time. They are "slimed" by the heavy energy around them. We are all sensitive deep down and are affected by the tone and quality of energy we find ourselves in. That's why we need to recognize how energy affects us and, more important, be discerning about what energy we allow to affect us.

The good news, however, is that you can protect yourself from such psychic contamination. The first line of defense is to acknowledge the nature of the psychic energy you are subjected to. The second is to allow yourself to walk away from the negative energy that doesn't feel good—and fast. Just feign illness or say you need some fresh air. You do. Realistically, however, you cannot always do that, such as when talking to your toxic boss, so here are other, more subtle ways to protect yourself.

The first is to decide to mind your own business and not that of others. This is one of the first lessons my teacher Charlie taught me. He wasn't admonishing me at the time. Instead, he was helping me avoid absorbing what I didn't want by keeping my attention solely on what my responsibilities were. "If someone is having a bad day," he'd advise, "stay away if possible and don't try to fix it. Trust that person will work it out. They usually do if you don't interfere." It was the best advice he ever gave me and the foundation of having good boundaries.

Second, get clear about your priorities and goals. The more defined your aims are, the more likely you will avoid psychic pollution from others. Remind yourself to observe, not absorb the energy around you, and refuse to take on energy that doesn't belong to you, doesn't serve you, or could harm you. The clearer your intentions and priorities are, the better your intuitive GPS will work and the more insulated you'll be from unwanted influences, as they will not be a vibrational match with your focus.

Third, consciously establish your energetic boundaries. You can easily become saturated with unwanted energy if you have wide-open intuitive channels and do not protect yourself by knowing and enforcing your boundaries. Unfortunately, I'm susceptible to this myself, so I must keep reminding myself, again and again, to keep my goals and priorities in mind and my energetic boundaries in place so I avoid sponging up other people's funky, low-vibe frequency.

Fourth, keep your distance from people with bad vibes, just as you would avoid someone with the flu. If someone is obviously throwing off bad energy, it's fine to feel compassion for them, but stand clear. Even though this is basic common sense, I must also remind myself to do this. For example, when I'm around a stressed, miserable person I love and am not grounded in my own body and clear about my priorities, I absorb their anxiety in about three minutes. It's like catching a psychic virus. Then we are both upset, and a fight or argument usually ensues, which helps no one. It's worse when I encounter someone with bad vibes I don't know. Having been taught to "be nice," I used to sit and take it. Not anymore. My new motto is "First and foremost, be nice to me." I suggest you adopt this rule as well.

For example, I recently got into a taxi in London, and the driver was in a terrible mood and had extremely negative energy, which hit me like a cloud of smoke. This surprised me, as the black cab drivers are usually some of the most wonderful, entertaining people I've encountered since moving here. Not so with this guy. Not today, anyway. He was dark, agitated, abrupt, and even scary. I rode with him for two blocks, then had enough. I didn't want him to ruin my day, so I said, "Excuse me, sir. I've changed my mind. Can you please let me out here?" His taxi was a swamp of bad vibes, and I wasn't going to suffer it for a minute longer. Annoyed, he pulled over, and I escaped as fast as possible. I had to walk a few blocks to clear my aura after that experience, but I succeeded, thank goodness. Remembering my instructions from Charlie, I refused to wonder why he was so toxic. It wasn't my business to know why or care. It was only my business to escape the bad vibes and care for myself.

Today's Jump Start

Observe but don't absorb the energy around you. If you find yourself in a toxic stew, walk away. If you can't do that, breathe slowly and exhale fully, releasing the poisonous or discordant energy as if mentally emptying the garbage. If the bad vibes are coming from someone you must interact with, turn your body slightly to either the right or left of the person and casually cross your arms slightly above your belly button. This is your solar plexus, the place in your body where you most easily absorb energy from around you.

Crossing your arms keeps you from absorbing energy. Continue to breathe slowly, inhaling mentally to the count of four, then exhaling to the count of four and completely emptying your body. Remain turned away with arms crossed and keep breathing for as long as you need to. This may be challenging when in the eye of someone's intense emotional storm, so it helps to practice beforehand when things are calm. That way, your body has already done this and will do so automatically again when needed.

DAY 17

Be Spontaneous

A student named Rosalie spontaneously enrolled in my intuition-development class without planning it in advance. When I asked how she came to be there, she said, "I'm not sure. I guess I just want to feel more intuitive, and this felt right." She shared that she had suffered an emotionally and physically abusive childhood that made her doubt her intuition. Finally, after years of therapy, Rosalie understood why she felt so disconnected from her true Self but was no closer to being guided from within than before. Or so she thought.

I admired that Rosalie signed up for my class and assured her she was wrong about feeling her intuition was not working. It was her intuition, after all, that brought her to me that very day. "Intuition doesn't always show up as an inner voice speaking clearly in your ear like you expect it should, Rosalie," I explained. "In fact, it often shows up as a more subtle force coming from deep within and moves your body without saying a single word or having a thought cross your mind. It often just moves you to do things you don't think about, just as it did when getting you here today." I then asked Rosalie if she could recall other times when she found herself spontaneously moved in a way she had not planned on or thought about in advance yet turned out to be positive for her.

She brightened and said, "Yes, when I met my husband."

"What happened?" I asked, curious to know more.

I was pushing a huge cart of pet supplies for my dog kennel business toward my car after having just left the pet-supply store, lost in my thoughts, when suddenly I bumped my cart into a guy heading my way. Horrified that I didn't see him coming, I apologized every which way. Still, in the back of my mind, it felt as if my cart had had a mind of its own, and I meant to hit him. I was relieved and surprised when he was so good-natured about it instead of getting angry with me. In fact, he took the cart and walked it and me to my car. After loading my three huge bags of dog food into the trunk, he asked me why I had so much dog food. I told him I ran a kennel. He said that was his dream. To make a long story short, he came often to the kennel after that,

*and over time we became friends. Now we are married and run
the kennel together. He talks to the people. I take care of the
dogs. We would never have met if my cart hadn't run into him.*

After listening to this delightful story, I pointed out to
Rosalie that her intuition worked just fine, nudging her
body in specific directions instead of talking in her ear. As
she considered this, it was as if a light bulb turned on in
her awareness:

*Now that I think of it, getting nudged often happens to me.
It's how I started my kennel business in the first place. I was
going to visit a friend when I drove by the kennel alongside the
highway. Spontaneously and without thinking, I pulled off and
went inside. I didn't even know why. I wasn't looking for a dog,
although I love them. I already had two. Once inside, I began
chatting with the owner, the sweetest older woman, who told me
she loved the kennel but wanted to sell it and retire. Before I
knew what was happening, I offered to buy it. I thought I was
crazy making that offer on the spot, but I didn't care. It felt
right. I didn't even get scared. It was as if it was meant for me to
drive there that day and take over. The woman who owned the
kennel still works there, teaching me all I need to know about
the business. I can't believe how fast it happened and how happy
I am that it did.*

When she was finished telling these stories, I pointed out
how all these events were examples of her intuition leading

her life. Rosalie laughed out loud and said, "I guess you're right. My intuition is working. I just didn't see it that way."

How about you? Can you recall any time you spontaneously let your inner guidance move you in a way that was out of character, without thought, or not in your plans? Did this prove to be a positive choice? More important, have you ever been nudged to move in a direction other than your planned course of action, but because it wasn't in your plans, you ignored it, only to regret it later?

My client John was going to work one morning when he suddenly felt a strong urge to pull over and check his tires. The impulse made no sense. Besides, he reasoned, if he followed it, he would be late for work, so he didn't. Unfortunately, shortly after getting on the highway, a tire on the semitruck right in front of him exploded, and a huge piece of it hit his windshield and shattered it, causing John to nearly lose control of the car and have a deadly accident. Luckily, he managed to maneuver his vehicle to the side of the road without hitting anyone. His car was severely damaged, but fortunately he survived. As John recounted the story, shaking his head introspectively, he said, "I felt such a strong urge to pull over that morning, which I ignored. Had I listened to my intuition, I would have avoided that accident. In the end, there was nothing wrong with my tires, but there certainly was something wrong with the tire on the semitruck pulling in front of me five minutes later."

John and Rosalie are not exceptional in being intuitively moved toward their highest good. If anything, this is the most powerful way your intuition communicates. People report feeling intuitive impulses that make no logical sense all the time. But because these impulses do not come with rational explanations, they generally get ignored. And sadly the result is often regret.

The key to benefiting from intuitive nudges is to be flexible and agree to move toward your highest good without needing an explanation. Consider these nudges—the most natural thing in the world—gifts, because they are. Be prepared to receive these nudges, and do not allow your intellect to stop you, demanding a logical explanation for what it cannot possibly understand before it agrees, or you'll miss the gift.

Today's Jump Start

Be open, receptive, spontaneous, and flexible today. Expect your intuition to move you. Before you head out the door, stretch in all directions, side to side, front and back, and in circles. Swivel your hips, swing your arms, roll your neck, bend your knees, and open your mind. Add a little music and dance to really get in the flow. Be mentally available to all intuitive impulses that may move you without the need for a logical explanation. The reason simply is "My intuition leads me toward my highest good, and I'm going with it." If you're a controlling person, this might be a little crazy-making, so approach this day playfully instead of fighting it. Breathing deeply and often helps you to remain open and flexible, so set a gentle alarm on your smartphone to ring every hour or so, reminding you to take a deep breath and stretch.

Today's practice invites you to be less mentally controlling and robotic and more spontaneous and receptive to the support of the Universe. Be curious and see where you end up today by setting the intention of allowing your Higher Self to move you toward your highest good. Enjoy any unexpected positive and pleasant surprises. Intuition is not something you can harness or control. It is the dynamic flow of Spirit through your body, overriding your intellect and carrying you on to the best possible wavelength of energy available to you today.

DAY 18

Laugh

Here's a quick, easy way to jump-start your intuitive super sense: laugh. Laughing quiets your ego and automatically turns on your sixth sense. Laughing catches your ego off guard and gives it a break from defending and protecting itself. When you laugh, you instantly jump up to a higher vibration, immediately receiving guidance and direction from your Spirit and from Spirit helpers that your ego simply has no access to.

The minute you begin laughing, your Spirit takes over. You override your ego, open your mind, and become available to new information that your ego will have missed or dismissed. Laughing not only elevates your awareness to a higher frequency but also clears your aura, gives you confidence, and sheds light on dark places in your mind. It's as good if not better than meditation for easing anxiety and freeing yourself of fear and doubt. When you laugh hard, you gain freedom from your ego and fully embody your Spirit.

Nothing has control over you if you can laugh at it. Laughter helps you forget your troubles, even for a moment, and when that happens, negativity, confusion, and anger disappear. Years ago, one of my master teachers taught me that "laughter chases the devil away"—the "devil" being any illusion, doubt, fear, or confusion that scares you, blocks answers, keeps you stuck, or causes you to question your fundamental safety, worthiness, and goodness. Laughter prevents you from taking yourself or life too seriously, removing this massive obstacle to receiving inner guidance. Your "serious" or intellectual Self is your ego, relentlessly trying to stay in charge and generally not open to spontaneity. In contrast, your Spirit is more lighthearted and playful. When you laugh, you let your Spirit take over and give your ego a break.

Years ago, I taught an intuitive development workshop at the Omega Institute in Rhinebeck, New York. For some reason, the students in this group took themselves way too seriously for their own good; consequently, most had little luck tapping into their sixth sense. So I encouraged them to make one another laugh to help them move out of this blocked state.

At first, they thought this was a stupid idea, but after much cajoling, they gave in and tried. They were a little rusty and not very funny initially, but eventually the participants loosened up and became more amusing. Some started crossing their eyes and making funny faces. Others pretended to be animals, hopping on one foot, making silly noises, and acting like a group of crazed kindergartners. The longer they tried, the funnier they became, until genuine hilarity caught on, making them laugh even more. For 15 minutes, everyone was so consumed with the Spirit of lighthearted silliness that I could barely get them to stop.

Once they'd calmed down, I invited them to try again to exercise their intuitive muscles. Much to their amazement, in this freer, playful state of being, they could successfully see their way out of problems they didn't think had solutions only minutes before. Their intuitive super sense instantly activated and allowed each student to describe one another's homes, jobs, secret heart desires, travel plans, and even great loves, although they were strangers who had just met. No one remained blocked, even the most doubting of Thomases among them. They were pretty stunned at how quickly a little humor jump-started their intuition and got it working to such a high degree. I wasn't. I've witnessed for years the power of laughter and how far it goes toward shedding light on answers to problems and illuminating the way forward when you initially feel stuck.

My client Jesse and his girlfriend, Bev, were two miserable people, arguing over money and how to pay their bills and how they both hated their restaurant jobs and wanted to quit. One night, instead of staying home and arguing as usual, they met old college friends for bowling at a '50s-style alley instead. They had so much fun that night, laughing for hours and hours, that by the end of the evening, both Jesse and Bev had forgotten their problems and were happier with one another and life than they had been in ages.

As they brushed their teeth before bed, Jessie was suddenly inspired and said, "I have an idea. Let's start a food truck and sell pancakes on a stick," a breakfast they had created together and both loved. Bev nearly screamed in agreement and was all in. They stayed up all night brainstorming about how to get started. Their ideas poured in "like pancake batter," Jesse said, one clever idea flowing in after another. Both Bev and Jesse intuitively knew this idea would work the more they joked and played and got sillier and sillier. In a matter of hours, they had downloaded their entire business plan.

They were even more enthusiastic about their idea the next day than the night before. Jesse called a few friends, and Bev called her parents. Everyone agreed to help. Three months later, Jesse and Bev were in business with a food truck called Sweet Cakes, parked near a corporate campus in Seattle. They were an instant hit. Jesse and Bev went from being miserable at work and with one another to having a fulfilling and fun shared purpose in life. It just took a few hours of laughing with friends to jump-start their super senses and get the inspiration they so desperately needed to find their way forward. It's not that having fun made any of this easy. They worked harder than ever to make their dream happen. But having fun turned on their inner light and illuminated their darkened outlooks, showing them the way forward. It was so clear that they knew they would succeed and did.

My first spiritual teacher, Charlie Goodman, was the one who tipped me off that laughter was the front door to my super sense. When I studied with him, he sometimes made me laugh so hard that tears ran down my cheeks. "No matter what you see or feel," he'd emphasize, "always keep a sense of humor about it." My mother said it her way: "The situation may be critical, but it's never serious."

In over 50 years of teaching the intuitive arts, I've found that the more I look for humor, the more I see Divine Spirit lighting the way. Cultivating our sense of humor increases our intuition and, as a bonus, improves our health. If we become too self-absorbed and serious about our problems, we lose touch with our super sense and our Spirit, making everything look dark. Laughter escorts us back to our true selves and back to life.

Today's Jump Start

Laugh today. Make it your top priority. Discover what tickles your funny bone and use it as much as possible. What funny animal and baby videos are on YouTube or TikTok? Tune in to the satellite comedy channel in your car instead of the news. If you're feeling depressed or don't feel like laughing, fake it. Tune in to a silly TV program or two to change your mental channel from worry to whimsy. This works well too.

Laughing chases away the dark shadows of life and instantly raises your vibration to a more balanced, relaxed, confident state. It reconnects you with your Spirit and gives your ego a break. The less you want to laugh, the more you need to. This is because you fear less what you laugh about. You may even overcome your fear altogether. After a day of laughter, check in with your super sense for solutions to your problems. Because you'll be more receptive after you've laughed a bit, I'm sure you will find them.

DAY 19

Ask Your Spirit

I grew up in a supersensory home where inner guidance was not considered a sixth sense. Instead, it was recognized as the first and most important of all our senses and the one to rely on in life no matter what. This conviction was passed on to us by my mother, a highly intuitive and creative artist and child war bride who survived the Holocaust. Separated from her family at 12 years old in an evacuation from her home in Romania in an air raid during World War II, my mom ended up in a German work camp until she was 14 and was liberated by American soldiers in 1945. She insisted that her intuition, which she called her Spirit, helped her survive the camp and go on to have a beautiful life. She also said her Spirit guided her to my father, a liberating American soldier who arrived in the town where she lived and whom she ultimately married at 16. Together and pregnant, they set sail for America. Eventually, six other children came along, with me among them, and I was named after her.

Amid the many traumas my mom suffered during those war years was a bout of rheumatic fever, which left her 95 percent deaf in both ears. However, instead of considering this a disability, she viewed her hearing loss as the greatest blessing of her life because, as she put it, "I don't have to listen to the negativity or craziness of people around me. The only thing I hear is the voice of my Spirit, which guides me beautifully every day." And it did.

Whenever she had to decide on something, my mom would close her eyes, turn her attention inward, listen to her inner voice, then announce, "My Spirit says..." and fill in the blank. And she followed those instructions without fail. So strongly did she value her inner voice for guidance that she insisted we do the same. Whenever one of my siblings or I asked my mom a question, her response was, "Before I answer, ask your Spirit. What does it say?" That simple question guided us inward for answers from the beginning. It was the most empowering gift she could have given us, laying the foundation for my life's work and purpose.

Our main family conversations centered on the question "What does your Spirit say?" We always asked ourselves and one another this question, and we still do.

We consider what the Spirit within says as our ultimate authority because it is. By consulting your Spirit, you stop turning to your ego to think, figure things out, worry, or control you with fear. Instead, you tap directly into your inner source of strength, quickly guiding you to the next steps leading toward your highest good. In asking your Spirit to guide you and then verbalizing what your Spirit suggests, you affirm your highest personal power and avoid the confusion and mistakes of letting your ego or other people take over your life.

Asking, "What does my Spirit say?" asserts your authority over your life and reminds you to check in with your intuition first and foremost. This is where you find the answers you seek, the ones that will take care of you best.

Because it was natural for me to ask, "What does my Spirit say?" I often ask my friends this same question whenever they are troubled. I remember asking this of my best girlfriend, Vickie, back in eighth grade when she told me her parents were getting a divorce, and she didn't know what to do. At first she looked confused and said, "What do you mean? I don't know what you're talking about." I explained that we all have a Spirit that gives us all the answers we need. Didn't she know that? I also explained that she needed to say whatever her Spirit suggested out loud, placing her hand on her heart. Once she announced her Spirit's answer out loud, she would have to listen to what it said.

I told Vickie she would feel peaceful if her Spirit responded when she asked for guidance. That's how she would know she was listening to the right channel. Your Spirit calms your body with its helpful guidance. However, you won't feel this calm if your ego is pretending to be your Spirit. Instead, you will feel agitated and restless and, underneath it all, unsafe.

Vickie was so fascinated by what I shared with her that day that this was all we talked about for months. Asking her Spirit for guidance worked. It got her through her parents' divorce and opened her up to a love of journaling and much more. Asking her Spirit for guidance and sharing what her Spirit said out loud gave Vickie a compass to guide her forward. It also gave her courage and confidence and kept her true to herself.

Vickie went on to study spirituality and metaphysics later in life and eventually became a meditation teacher. She often said learning to ask her Spirit for guidance out loud that day we talked was a turning point in her life. "I could have been a drug addict or worse," she said. "My dad was a drug addict, and my mom had no self-esteem, so they couldn't guide me in any way because they were both messes. My Spirit took over and helped me where they failed. I got through my adolescence relatively intact by asking my Spirit to lead the way."

Today's Jump Start

Let your Spirit lead today. Ask your Spirit what to do every time you face a decision today, from where to park the car to where to find your house keys to your life's purpose. Before each ask, take a deep breath and get grounded in your body. Check in to see if you are genuinely available to receive an honest response. Then pose your question quickly and clearly and let your Spirit answer aloud, "My Spirit says...," and quickly fill in the blank.

This trains you to turn your life over to your inner guidance and put your ego in the background. Ask your Spirit for guidance at least five times today, or more if needed.

DAY 20

Walk on It

Every day I take long walks and have since I was a child. Now that I live mainly in London, I am blessed to walk through Regent's Park near me, one of the most stunning open spaces in this city and the home to over 410 acres of wildlife and gardens. Coming from Chicago, primarily an urban mass of gray with bitterly cold temperatures for most of the year, I am amazed at the gift of this expansive, beautiful sanctuary of burgeoning nature near my front door.

My daily walks offer more than physical exercise. They are my time to connect with my Spirit, listen to my soul, check in with my body, tune in to my intuition, and receive guidance, inspiration, and answers to my life's most challenging questions. The hour I spend wandering through the trees, strolling near the zoo, observing the geese, ducks, and more exotic fowl in the water and seeing and hearing the beautiful birds soaring through the trees takes me to heaven and back. Walks in nature soothe my frayed nerves and calm my body. The green surrounding me gets me out of my head and connects me to the earth. By the time I return home, I feel restored and clear. My nervous system is reset. I sense my true rhythm.

When I lived in Paris, I walked daily along the Seine River, which snakes down the city's center from one end to the other. I'd start at Pont de l'Alma near the Eiffel Tower, walk to Notre-Dame, and then walk back. The entire journey took about an hour and was exquisite. My walk was an opportunity to use movement and beauty to help me connect to my Spirit and receive the inner guidance I needed for that day.

Since I was very young, walking has been one of the most powerful means of sharpening my super sense, tuning out the noisy world, and returning to the center of my heart and Spirit. Walking is medicine, and walking anywhere works when I need guidance. In fact, whenever I felt stuck, my mom used to say, "Don't talk about it. Walk on it!" It's nature's therapy and brings about potent relief for overthinking and anything else that ails you.

Moving my feet, one after the other, for an extended time quiets the internal noise that comes from being overwhelmed, overstimulated, overspent, and oversaturated, all the things life leaves you feeling these days.

My teacher Charlie once explained how vital walking was to the mystic and intuitive after I shared how much I loved walking to his house for our weekly lesson instead of riding my bike or taking the bus. He said when you walk, your angels and guides walk with you. When you move your body in this rhythmic way, your ego goes to sleep so you can hear your angels, guides, and Higher Self. He was right. That is precisely what happens when I go for long walks. "If you need help, go for a walk with heaven, and you'll get it," he assured me.

Charlie's emphasis on the power of walking for intuitive guidance left such an impression on me that when my father and brother died and my husband of 32 years suddenly left all in the span of six weeks, I intuitively felt that the only way I was ever going to heal was to walk the Camino de Santiago, a 500-mile pilgrimage from France to Spain. There was no question I would go. I had to.

This experience was so therapeutic and profoundly healing that I even wrote a book about it—*Walking Home: A Pilgrimage from Humbled to Healed*. On that 35-day walk across two mountain ranges and a desert, I was guided to gather my broken pieces and begin a new life. If I had not gone on that pilgrimage, I wouldn't have recovered from the devastation of losing my father, brother, and husband within six weeks as fast as I did. At the time, I felt my life was over, but as I walked, the vision for the next chapter of my life appeared as a huge surprise. I am confident that guidance on what to do after so much grief and loss would never have come to me had I chosen to sit and dwell on my losses instead of getting moving. Walking took me out of the past and pushed me into the future.

The French understand the power of the walk for connecting to the Spirit. They even have a word for a walker. It's "flâneur" or "flâneuse," meaning someone who strolls around the city streets, observing and experiencing the urban environment without any destination or purpose. A flâneur recognizes the healing quality of the stroll, as well as the discovery it brings with it, another element that feeds intuition. When you walk as a flâneur or flâneuse, you relax the mind, and it opens to new ideas. Walking introduces unique scenery outside and inside. Strolling, the best intuitive walking, loosens fixed ideas and shakes up old beliefs and perspectives. It also allows your inner guidance to bring you surprises.

My friend Maureen visited me in Paris several years ago and, upon my urging, spent the day wandering about on foot, discovering the city without a guidebook. She started out at the Sacré-Coeur in the north of Paris and quickly ended up in an area near Château d'Eau, which she had been advised by friends in Maryland to avoid at all costs because it was so dangerous. At first Maureen felt scared when she realized where she was, but the sights and sounds were fabulous, and nothing terrible happened. Soon her fears gave way to pleasure at the charm and excitement of all she was discovering. Maureen was guided to a particular bead shop as she "flâneused" her way along, and once she entered, she met the kindest woman, Ima, from Morocco, who offered her tea. No longer scared and in no hurry, Maureen accepted the kind offer and stayed for hours, promising to return soon. And she did. Maureen returned twice, receiving a dinner invitation to meet Ima's family the last time she showed up.

To make a long story short, Maureen and Ima became great friends. Five years later, they are still friends, and Maureen is planning a monthlong vacation with Ima in Morocco this fall. Her walk led her to what she was really looking for when she started out that day—meaningful connections and real adventures. That is what an intuitive walk always brings with it.

Today's Jump Start

Today take a break from your routine and go for a long walk, either in the morning, for example, on your way to work, or in the evening, on the way home from work. If time and responsibility don't allow for a long walk, adjust your schedule and walk for 10 to 15 minutes around the neighborhood. For example, if driving home from work, park your car and walk around the block twice before entering the door. Do the same if going to work. Leave early so you can park and walk before entering the building. Another alternative is to get up earlier and walk in a nearby park before heading off to work.

If possible, walk in nature. If that is not possible, notice nature wherever you are. Notice the trees, gardens, grass, birds, flowers, and clouds. Nature gets you out of your head, healing the body and quickly attuning you to your heart and intuition. Listen to the world around you with your entire body as you walk. Follow your vibes as you go. If the direction in which you are walking feels good, continue. If you get bad vibes, reverse, turn around, and change directions fast.

You can also activate your intuition by exploring an unfamiliar area. Be the flâneur or flâneuse and have an adventure for an hour or so without a destination. Let your Spirit lead the way as you wander, being open and spontaneous. If you get an intuitive hit to enter a shop or follow a particular path, for example, don't hesitate. Check it out. Be aware of your Higher Self and Divine support system walking with you.

If you are struggling with a problem, ask your Higher Self to help you solve it as you walk. Then, challenging as it may be, don't think about it as you walk. Take your mind off the problem by noticing and enjoying the world around you as you stroll. Stop and notice details. Listen to the sounds all around. Are there birds? Is there wind? Are there kids playing? Dogs barking? Trees rustling? Feel the elements on your skin. Is it cold, fresh, warm? It is calm? How about the smells? Do you smell flowers, trees, exhaust fumes, food?

Check in with all your senses as you walk and be fully in your body and the present moment. This clears your mind so intuition can find its way to your attention. Walking moves your energy from the problem state to the solution state, so this simple action frees our mental blocks and naturally opens the door to intuitive guidance. Answers may not show up on the walk, but they will pop up soon after. Follow your impulses and listen to your intuition as you stroll along. Talk to your Spirit and ask to receive inspiration and guidance as you go. Be open to having a great intuitive adventure. You will not be disappointed.

DAY 21

Find 19 Solutions

Over the many years of teaching and training people to activate their intuition, I've noticed a distinct difference between those who succeed and those who don't. The ones who fully expect to discover solutions to their problems will succeed, while those who focus only on problems won't. Some even go so far as to refuse to consider solutions when they are offered.

Problems are the ego's favorite thing because they give it a reason for existing. A problem confirms the ego's primary point of view in life: "Life is out to get me, so be prepared for the worst at all times." This point of view keeps the ego fighting its life, its favorite pastime. Many people have become so disconnected from their Spirit that they erroneously believe their ego to be their only Self, and the ego wants to keep it that way.

On the other hand, intuitive people recognize themselves as more than only ego. They know themselves as spiritual beings in a loving, unlimited, and supportive Universe. They recognize their ego to be their limited false Self, a helper, at best, to their Spirit but not the leader of their lives. Their strong connection to Universal guidance creates an entirely different reality: one in which we are here to create meaningful, purposeful lives filled with joy and where the Universe is always available to help us succeed by communicating through our intuition.

The funny thing is that both types of people are correct; they just have different experiences. Unlike ego-driven people who are fear-based and limited and therefore focus on problems and threats, intuitive people know there's always a solution to every problem, no matter how complex or challenging, and love to discover it. So, acting like Divine detectives, they watch out for every clue, no matter how subtle or seemingly insignificant, knowing it will help lead to the answers they seek. Exclusively ego-driven people also get to be right in not finding a solution if they are convinced there isn't one and refuse to consider looking for it. In either world, you are right. But in the ego-driven world, you lock yourself out from the gifts and joy that all those wonderful solutions offer.

My mom introduced the "there's always a solution" outlook when I was young. In our home, problems without solutions simply did not exist. Every problem, big or small, was merely an invitation to use our intuition and creativity. My mom's absolute conviction that there is always a solution settled into my DNA and was reinforced with each miracle we experienced, and they were nonstop.

My first direct experience in finding a solution to a seemingly insurmountable problem occurred when I was eight years old and wanted to win a prize from Santa as he drove around town in Denver, where we lived at the time. The way to get a slim shot at the gift was to create the most beautiful sign for Santa to see, put it in your front window, and hope he'd drive by and like it. Frustrated by my poor odds as I created my amateur sign, I told my mom I had little hope. However, she wouldn't hear my negative outlook. "Don't focus on your competition. Create the sign with the expectation to win, and you will," she insisted. And that was that as far as she was concerned. Thanks to our conversation, I stopped focusing on the odds against me and thought only about winning as I colored away. The next day, I won my first color-console TV just in time for Christmas. From that day forward, there has never been a problem I felt I couldn't solve or would not find an answer to.

My teacher Charlie took the concept of always finding a solution to a whole new level when he taught me that every problem had not one but 19 possible solutions. Moreover, a master intuitive person, he insisted, should consider all 19 solutions before choosing the best one. One of my regular assignments as Charlie's apprentice was finding 19 solutions to various problems presented by people who had written to him asking for his help. It was my favorite part of my apprenticeship and was tremendous fun.

Once, I asked Charlie, "What if I'm wrong?"

"Right and wrong are subjective ideas, Sonia," he replied. "What is right for one person might not be for another. Better focus on what feels true for you for now and not worry about being wrong."

Teaching me there's always a solution and then suggesting that there are 19 solutions, not one, to every problem has laid the foundation for me to have an unstoppable and enormously creative approach to life. The only other thing necessary to integrate this perspective is having a tremendous sense of humor as you search for answers. And one more piece of advice: be willing to be surprised.

I consulted with a 69-year-old librarian, Denise, who came for an intuitive reading, distraught beyond consolation over being forced into early retirement. Panicked and afraid she'd run out of money before she lived out her life, Denise could see no solution going forward. Her entire sense of security was based solely on the paycheck she was used to receiving, and now that that was going to be cut off, she only saw destitution.

I tried to reassure Denise that she would soon be working again, but she could not hear it. She refused to believe me. "No one would want me at my age," she argued. Using the 19 solutions technique in her reading, I shared multiple options to find income as she moved ahead, but she batted each one away like an unwanted fly. Her ego was enjoying her panic attack way too much to listen.

Denise left more miserable than when she came. However, a week later, she was unexpectedly offered a job in a new mobile library that opened in town, something she had never even heard of. Her old boss offered her this job the minute it came up because she had been troubled by having to let Denise go so suddenly. The bookmobile job provided Denise with enough to pay her tiny monthly mortgage, insurance, and food bill without touching a penny of her retirement money. Denise was flabbergasted that a solution came to her without her even trying to find one. She returned to ask me about the other 18 solutions I had tried to share with her.

I asked her why she was interested since her problem was solved. She said she would like to teach the kids and students who came to her mobile library how to look for 19 solutions when they faced a problem so they wouldn't ever feel panicked and backed into the corner as she had felt. Denise became a local legend for the 19 solutions game happening in the bookmobile. Soon everybody in town was becoming more intuitive and creative thanks to this previous skeptic now spreading the word.

Today's Jump Start

Today you are going to flex your intuitive muscles and wake up your imagination at the same time by playing 19 solutions. You can do this alone or with a partner, as you choose. If you decide to work with a partner, only ask someone willing to be a good sport and be open to the process while having fun with it.

Begin by writing down a problem for which you have no immediate solution, causing you to be worried or anxious or feel threatened in some way. Then either by writing them down or counting them off with a friend, immediately start naming 19 solutions to this problem. Your solutions can be practical or wildly creative and unrealistic. The point of this game is not to figure out an answer intellectually but to let your imagination wake up your intuition and surprise you with solutions your intellect or ego would never have considered.

The key to success is to respond as fast as possible, spending no more than 30 seconds to come up with each solution. The only other rule is to not repeat a solution once you have named it. The magic of this game is that by the time you get to the 19th solution, you will have discovered at least two or three real solutions that will work. You will know this by the big happy smile and sense of relief crossing your face and running through your body.

If you're playing this game with a friend, you can take turns instead of going back and forth, each one naming a problem and all 19 solutions before the other person begins. You can apply 19 solutions to as many problems as you want. In fact, the more problems you present, the merrier, because with each one, your intuition and creativity get a significant workout. This effort makes them both strong and reliable.

Afterword

Now that you've jump-started your intuition, I hope you enjoy the endless gifts this super sense brings into your life. If you feel, however, even after doing the jump-starts these past three weeks that you're not yet fully confident in your intuition, simply go back to the beginning of this book and practice the jump-starts all over again. Doing this will further strengthen your intuition and help reanchor it into your life as intended. You can never practice these jump-start tools enough! They are designed to become your natural way of life. After reviewing this book a few times, keep it in view and pick it up often. Randomly open the book to any page and practice the jump start you find there. Each jump-start is like a little psychic sit-up: the more you practice, the stronger your intuitive muscles become. Before you know it, your intuition will be up and running like the super sense it is, bringing you fun, flow, and fulfillment. In fact, you'll wonder how you ever got along without it!

All my love, *Sonia*

About the Author

Sonia Choquette is celebrated worldwide as an author, spiritual teacher, and intuitive guide who has devoted herself to teaching people to honor their Spirit, trust their vibes, and live in the grace and glory of an extraordinary Spirit-guided life.

A fourth-generation intuitive guide, beginning her public work with Spirit at age 15, Sonia has spent over 45 years traveling the world on her mission to help others lead confident, authentic lives with intuition as their guiding light. She is the author of 27 internationally best-selling books and numerous audio programs on intuitive awakening, personal and creative growth, and spiritual transformation.

Sonia's work has been published in over 40 countries and translated into 37 languages, making her one of the most widely read authors and experts in her field of work.

www.soniachoquette.net

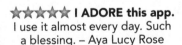

CONNECT WITH
HAY HOUSE
ONLINE

🌐 hayhouse.co.uk   **f** @hayhouse

📷 @hayhouseuk   **X** @hayhouseuk

▶ @hayhouseuk   ♪ @hayhouseuk

Find out all about our latest books & card decks • Be the first to know about exclusive discounts • Interact with our authors in live broadcasts • Celebrate the cycle of the seasons with us • Watch free videos from your favourite authors • Connect with like-minded souls

'The gateways to wisdom and knowledge are always open.'

Louise Hay